W9-DEA-770

Globalization and the Environment

SUNY series in Global Politics
James N. Rosenau, editor

A complete listing of books in this series can be found at the end of this volume.

Globalization and the Environment

Greening Global Political Economy

Gabriela Kütting

CABRINI COLLEGE LIBRARY
610 KING OF PRUSSIA RD.
RADNOR. PA 19087-3699

State University of New York Press

*#528 46532

Published by
State University of New York Press, Albany

© 2004 State University of New York

All rights reserved

Printed in the United States of America

No part of this book may be used or reproduced in any manner whatsoever
without written permission. No part of this book may be stored in a retrieval system
or transmitted in any form or by any means including electronic, electrostatic,
magnetic tape, mechanical, photocopying, recording, or otherwise
without the prior permission in writing of the publisher.

For information, address State University of New York Press,
90 State Street, Suite 700, Albany, N.Y., 12207

Production by Diane Ganeles
Marketing by Michael Campochiaro

Library of Congress Cataloging-in-Publication Data

Kütting, Gabriela, 1967–
    Globalization and the environment : greening global political economy / Gabriela Kütting.
        p. cm. — (SUNY series in global politics)
    Includes bibliographical references and index.
    ISBN 0-7914-6135-1 (alk. paper)
        1. Environmental economics. 2. Sustainable development. 3. Globalization. I. Title. II.
    Series.

HC79.E5K88 2004
338.9'27—dc22   2003061718

10 9 8 7 6 5 4 3 2 1

Contents

Preface   vii

Part I: The Conceptual Argument for Eco-Holistic Analysis

Chapter 1. A Critical Review of Global Political Economy
from an Eco-Holistic Perspective   3

Chapter 2. Linking Environment and Society   23

Chapter 3. Cultural versus Political Economy Approaches:
Production and Consumption   43

Chapter 4. Equity, Environment, and Global Political Economy   63

Part II: Eco-Holism in Practice

Chapter 5. The Political Economy of Garments,
Especially Cotton   87

Chapter 6. The Case of West Africa   107

Chapter 7. Conclusion   127

Bibliography   139

Index   155

SUNY series in Global Politics   163

Preface

This book critically examines the concept and processes of a globalizing political economy in relation to environmental and social concerns. Globalization both as a concept and as a process is a contested term—its usage has become generally accepted but there is no definition of what constitutes globalization and its empirical features. Attempts at conceptualizing or theorizing about globalization from an international political economy (IPE) perspective tend to sideline the environmental and social consequences of globalization and these issues are usually treated as part of an analysis of global civil society and new social movements. However, in such a context only transnational actors representing social and environmental issues are incorporated into the analysis rather than the structural and systemic forces and constraints within which actors operate. This book aims to address this gap in the literature by offering a conceptual analysis of the social relations between the various actors in the global system and in the structural environment in which they operate.

In order to advance any debate about environment and the globalizing political economy, inroads need to be made into a definition of the term globalization. This will be the first task of the book. This book will be based on the argument that globalization is not a fundamentally new concept in history but is the latest variant of an inherently globalizing political economy. Much has been written about the trade and financial aspects of globalization in IPE. Likewise, transnational agency has been widely researched. The negative social and environmental consequences of globalization have also been publicized, albeit mostly from an agency perspective. The aim of this book is to unite and embed these concerns in a holistic conceptual framework.

This will be achieved in the following way: First, the debate about the definition of globalization will be summarized and critically evaluated. This introductory debate will be followed by a summary of the most prevalent theoretical approaches to global/international political economy and their conceptual shortcomings with regard to weaving in an eco-holistic perspective into mainstream approaches. Therefore chapter 1 will be a review of core IPE/GPE (global political economy) approaches and their environmental components. The term eco-holistic is a new concept, denoting the need to merge the concerns of both holistic and ecocentric approaches. Holistic approaches have traditionally been focused on traditional social science, incorporating social, political, and economic factors but have not usually included environmental criteria. Ecocentric approaches, on the other hand, focus on the ecological aspect of analysis, thus usually subordinating the social, political and economic angle. The term eco-holistic emphasizes that analysis will be social, political, economic, *and* environmental. Chapter 1 subjects the mainstream global political economy approaches to such eco-holistic analysis. It reviews liberal and historical materialist approaches to GPE and globalization. It also looks at the ever-increasing literature coming from an anti-globalization and environmentalist perspective and tries to incorporate this into more structured analysis.

The remainder of the book is aimed at introducing new concepts to the construction of the globalizing political economy on the basis of an eco-holistic perspective. This concept will be built around three pillars. The three pillars are the historical dimension of environment and society relations, the concept of consumption, and the concept of equity. It is argued that a more inclusive and eco-holistic approach should include aspects of all three pillars.

Chapter 2 outlines the concept of an eco-holistic approach with a historical discussion of environment-society relations, referring to time-space distanciation, the understanding of time in social relations, the historical dimension of the social relations of economy and the environment, as well as the lack of effectiveness in global governance. The social and structural origins of environmental degradation in a global political economy are discussed in detail in this chapter.

Chapter 3 discusses the cultural dimension of political economy with a particular focus on the institutions of production and consumption. The analysis and practice of GPE is heavily tilted toward an understanding of the processes of production and here the argument is made that for an eco-holistic and equitable understanding of GPE the institution of consumption needs to be equally studied and understood.

Chapter 4 develops the environmental critique of the global political economy of chapters 1–3 to include issues of equity and social justice. Environmental problems do not exist separately or in isolation from social problems. This chapter explores the connection between social and environmental consequences of globalization and addresses the inequitable distribution of power and wealth as well as questions of social justice and their compatibility with the neoliberal ideology underlying globalization. This chapter concludes section I.

Section II is aimed at exploring the concepts discussed in section I in an empirical context. The illustrative case study in question is the global cotton/garment chain. It has been selected because it is both underresearched and at the same time one of the most socially and environmentally degrading production/consumption chains in existence. This section will study the global political economy of cotton production and garment consumption from a historical perspective and trace the social and structural origins of degradation in a globalizing political economy. This will be followed by an illustrative case study, showing how global developments such as financial and trade liberalization as well as a global division of labor go hand in hand with changing consumption and fashion patterns in the North and have dramatic consequences for local agricultural, social, and environmental patterns in developing cotton producer states. The social and environmental consequences of the impact of such global trends will be discussed in relation to West Africa. West Africa, and Africa in general, are seen as outside the globalization remit due to a lack of economic development. However, in fact, Africa is very much part of a globalizing economy, albeit in a dependent relationship in the agricultural sector. Many countries in West Africa, for example, have dramatically increased their cotton production in the past five years to use the income from this cash crop for debt servicing, often with severe social and environmental consequences. Thus West Africa is seen as an excellent illustration for the issues discussed in this book. This section will then make specific international policy suggestions that will tackle the social and environmental degradation within the cotton chain. This analysis will lead to the conclusion that in a global political economy global as well as local or regional solutions will have to be found for problems that may only exist at the local level (but that have their structural origins elsewhere).

Chapter 5 looks at the global political economy of cotton production and garment consumption from a historical perspective, outlining the changes that have led to the globalizing of the forces of production and the role of consumption in the garment sector in the last stages of the twentieth century and the dramatic consequences this has had in the social and environmental field.

Particular attention will be given to the social and environmental effects of globalization in cotton production in developing countries in chapter 6. West Africa is a region that has massively expanded its cotton production in recent years in order to use this cash crop income to pay off its debts. This policy, arising out of its position in the global political economy, has had serious consequences in a social and ecological context. The linkages between these issues will be explored in this chapter. Thus this illustrative case study shows clearly how the local and global are connected over history. Historically, West Africa was a cotton-producing region under colonialism and many parallels can be drawn between the role of cotton in West Africa under colonialism and today. The relationship between outside powers shaping livelihoods in a predominantly agrarian society and the linkages to a globalizing political economy are explored here as well. These linkages can be traced back to the issues discussed in chapters 1–4, especially the relationship between production and consumption, and are particularly visible in the nature of the product cycle of textiles that start off their lives as raw materials within the region and return as commodities on the second-hand clothing market. Such a life cycle raises ethical, cultural, as well as environmental dimensions that are not necessarily the immediately obvious ones that are discussed in detail in this chapter. Above all, this illustrative case shows the necessity for IPE/GPE analysis on the basis of an eco-holistic approach as the multifaceted dimensions of these politico-economic relations cannot be grasped with neither traditional liberal nor traditional historical materialist approaches.

The social and environmental consequences of a globalizing political economy are not the 'careering juggernauts' Giddens (1990) refers to but can be regulated at the local, regional, international, and global level. Chapter 7 provides an overview of existing attempts at regulating these problems and makes further policy suggestions aimed at reversing the downward spiral of social rights and environmental degradation.

Many people have contributed to this project. As Visiting Research Fellow in the Political Science Department of Colorado State University I have benefited from invaluable library resources. I am grateful to Kathy Hochstetler, Michelle Betsil, Valerie Assetto, Steve Mumme, and most of all to Dimitris Stevis (who made this trip possible) for insightful comments on my work. Parts of this book have been presented as conference papers at the International Studies Association and at the British International Studies Association annual conferences. Marc Williams, Tom Princen, Tom Cioppa, Hans Bruyninckx, Lisa Dale, Catherine-Zoi Varfis, Ronnie Lipschutz, Sing Chew, Ho-Won Jeong, Martin Weber, Detlef Sprinz, Branwen Gruffydd Jones, John Vogler, Charlotte Bretherton, Peter Willetts, Gordon Davidson, Libby Assassi, and Peter Fuchs have all been extremely helpful. I am grateful to the Carnegie Trust for the Universities of Scotland for two travel grants, one for library research in South-East England and one that enabled me to undertake interviews in West Africa. I am also grateful to the Department of Politics and International Relations at Aberdeen for giving me the opportunity to use research income to partially buy myself out of teaching for a term to focus my attention entirely on this book project. Various non-government organizations have been incredibly helpful such as the Pesticides Trust, Oxfam, UK but most of all I would like to thank Père Maurice Oudet of Sedelan in Koudougou/Burkina Faso for his invaluable help and insights. I am grateful to Michael Rinella of State University of New York Press for his courteous, prompt, and efficient handling of the editorial process of this book. My greatest thanks go to Dimitris Stevis and Pam Shaw for spending inordinate amounts of time and energy in supporting me in pursuing this project.

Part I

The Conceptual Argument
for
Eco-Holistic Analysis

Chapter 1

A Critical Review of Global Political Economy from an Eco-Holistic Perspective

The subject of international or global political economy (IPE or GPE) has established itself as a core International Relations (IR) element in the past fifteen years. However, the IPE/GPE discourse and the environmental discourse within IR have more or less existed side by side and have not cross-fertilized despite obvious linkages. The aim of this chapter is to outline the environmental dimension of core IPE/GPE approaches or, in the absence of a clear environmental dimension, to analyze the potential for an environmental component of these approaches. Although the approach of this book is based on the concept of a global political economy, both the terms IPE and GPE shall be used for literature review purposes. As substantial parts of recent GPE writings have been subsumed under the umbrella of globalization, the topic of globalization will also be included in this analysis. This chapter provides an overview of the different approaches to, and theories of, globalization as the latest variant of GPE and assesses their usefulness in providing a holistic, including ecological, analysis of existing political economy trends under the new forms of economic organization that have come into being since the 1970s. Since this chapter serves as an introduction to both subject matters, it is kept necessarily basic so as to familiarize the IPE/GPE audience with environmental discourse and the environmental audience with IPE/GPE concerns.

There are no direct environmental approaches to IPE/GPE, which is a clear gap in the literature and this book is one attempt to fill this vacuum. There are many empirical accounts of the impact of certain aspects of GPE on the environment or of certain actors. However, none of this translates into a theory or a conceptual framework of environmental GPE although many of the existing GPE approaches could easily incorporate an environmental dimension if amended accordingly.

Empirical analyses of the environmental impact of GPE range from studies of the institutional frameworks set up to dealing with environmental problems to the analysis of particular problems and their direct origins. An example of the latter kind of study is Peter Dauvergne's analysis of the environmental consequences of loggers and degradation in the Asia-Pacific (2000) while examples of the former kind of literature would be analyses of World Bank or World Trade Organization (WTO) policies and how they relate to environmental degradation (Williams, 2001). Most environmental political economy analysis, however, can still be found in the field of regime-type studies of particular institutional frameworks that deal with environmental problems (Young, 1997; Haas, Keohane, & Levy, 1995).

This book will take a different angle and the critical review of GPE approaches in this chapter acts as an introduction to the conceptual framework that will be developed in chapters 2–4. First, reflecting on the growing importance of the process of globalization within GPE, is it possible to define the term globalization within global political economy? Given the widespread use of this term for the contemporary organization of the global political economy, its definition and a discussion of the validity of the concept is an obvious starting point for this review (and indeed for a book on environment and GPE). Then the chapter will address several schools of thought that have emerged as the predominant ones of the past decade, namely the historical approach, the liberal approach, and the globalization skeptics. In addition, environmental approaches to global political economy/globalization will be introduced and assessed in this context.

It is generally agreed that the 1970s have seen fundamental changes in the way in which the international political economy is organized, leading to a more global approach both in IPE/GPE and environment (Strange, 1996; Scholte, 1993; Mittelman, 1997; Lipschutz, 1996). What is debatable, however, is if these changes are deserving of the term globalization that they have been allocated. Among IPE/GPE scholars the age of globalization is taken to be the post-Fordist era that has engendered economics of flexibility, increasing trade liberalization, financial deregulation, an increasingly global division of labor, and a transnational capitalist class (Sklair, 1998; Lipiètz, 1997, Strange, 1996). Although the phenomenon of globalization itself is contested, these changes in the international political economy are not. So in a way there are two parallel debates about globalization as a phenomenon: whether it exists or not and whether the 1970s changes in the global/international political economy are a historically new phase or just a continuum of a historically rooted phenomenon (Hirst & Thompson, 1996; Schwartz, 2000).

The first debate, about whether these changes constitute globalization or not, is a definitional problem. By definition global means the encompassing of the whole globe rather than just certain regions. Therefore it would not be technically, geographically, or indeed spatially correct to use the term globalization for economic, social, or political phenomena that affect only part of the (inhabited) world as many authors do indeed propose. Globalization as opposed to internationalization also means that political and economic processes become truly global rather than just international or transnational, i.e. an international system inclusive of more actors than the state-centric view suggests—thus leading to a more pluralist, or globalist, weltanschauung. In terms of inclusiveness, globalization is a phenomenon that affects global society and not just a part of society or an elite. Global has to be truly inclusively global in order to justify the use of this drastic term. A cursory look at the contemporary political economy suggests that most political and economic processes fail the test of being global although in some economic sectors and especially in the division of labor there are certainly many global aspects in the organization of these phenomena. This means that to use the term globalization to describe the political and economic changes since the 1970s is an exaggeration and that we can only talk of partial globalization or of a globalizing process. This does not mean that globalization does not exist, only that it is not as pervasive and all-encompassing as it is usually presented. Thus it is more helpful to speak of a globalizing political economy rather than globalization.

The second point I want to emphasize, on the origins of globalization, is a question about both globalization and economic history. Some academics argue that globalization started with the formation of societies and with the social relations between them and that we have now entered a higher stage of a linear, historically determined process (Frank, 1998). Others would see globalization as coexisting with capitalism and again, depending on one's definition of capitalism and the different start dates that are given (Wallerstein, 1995; Cox, 1996; Altvater & Mahnkopf, 1999). This school of thought sees globalization as a higher or latest stage of capitalism. Last, some researchers would suggest that globalization and the socio-economic changes witnessed since the 1970s are an entirely new phenomenon that is separate from the other processes just mentioned (Cox, 1997; Mittelman, 1997).

Writers such as James Mittelman and Robert Cox focus on the economic side of globalization and see these economic changes as the driving factor behind other global changes. These economic changes are empirically observable phenomena and have altered the shape of the global political economy. In this view, these developments have also led to institutional developments, such as alterations in World Bank and International Monetary Fund (IMF) policies, changes in the General Agreement on Tariffs and Trade (GATT) and the establishment of the World Trade Organization, shifts in the way in which the United Nations is used as a political instrument by states and the rise of global civil society, as well as some changes in the role of the state in the international system. The beginning globalization of certain economic and financial sectors has surely had an impact on local organization as well (Hertel,

1996; Klak, 1998). However, it cannot be argued that these emerging processes have led to a fundamental reorganization of the international system and to the emergence of a global system. This is simply not the case. States are still the only sovereign actors in the international system and sanction fundamental changes. Their role has certainly changed over time and they are engaged in more consultation exercises and are more constrained in their choices, as are multilateral funding agencies (and also multilateral corporations). Nevertheless, the structural changes experienced over the past thirty years in the international system have not made states the servants of multinational corporations as is often maintained.

The structures of the international system have undeniably changed with the onset of the process of globalization that is witnessed by the establishment of the World Trade Organisation and by the changing role and rise in importance of the International Monetary Fund and the World Bank. These changes are linked to the breakdown of the Bretton Woods system and to the ensuing structural changes in production and finance (Cox, 1997). However, the fundamental structures of the system are still in place. The global political economy is still managed from the political and economic/financial centers of the world that are situated in developed countries and the underlying ideology of the international system is still by and large the same as well. The relationship between core and periphery has not fundamentally changed either. While some countries have made the transition from developing to developed countries, overall the world-system structures of core, periphery, and semiperiphery have not been affected by the onset of the process of globalization.

Therefore the fashionable argument about globalization being an entirely new phenomenon is discarded in this book. This approach is largely based on cultural and social ideas of globalization and on the reach of better transport and communication links that decrease physical and virtual distance between places and people. However, communication and travel methods have continuously improved during the course of history and there is no argument to suggest that the changes in the past thirty years are so fundamentally different from what existed before that they are deserving of an entirely new term. In addition, modern transport and communication means are only available to a relatively small elite of the world population and are by no means global in reach. Thus the *social relations* of transport and communication have not changed although the *spatial reach or speed* of these communications means has increased. Vast parts of developing countries do not have regular electricity supply or telephone access; therefore talking about a global village is an exaggeration. For example, in sub-Saharan Africa and in South Asia, only 14 to 15 telephone lines existed per 1,000 people in 1996 while 1.5 personal computers were counted per 1,000 people in South Asia (World Development Indicators/World Bank Atlas, 1998: 48–49). The world may be a global village for some but not for the vast majority of the population. Likewise, cultural linkages and a cultural melting pot are also largely a myth. There may be a case for a 'coca-colization' argument but this is limited to certain branded products that have global appeal. The internationalization of food is also something that is largely only available to an elite who can afford to frequent exotic restaurants. These are not global phenomena and they are also not new. They may be more widespread today but this increase in volume is not related to a fundamental change in social relations.

It is more difficult to decide whether globalization finds its roots in the advent of capitalism or if it is intrinsic in societal evolution. This also leads to debates about the nature of capitalism, whether to accept the notion that modern capitalism is unique or whether historically other societies intent on capital accumulation can also be described as capitalist. If the latter argument is accepted, then the two arguments of globalization as intrinsic in societal evolution and findings its roots in the advent of capitalism are not really all that different. Both accounts take a linear view of history and are based on the idea of continuous social progress and societal change and evolution. In this evolution, globalization is just the latest stage of development.

In some ways, it is irrelevant whether capitalism is a process that started in the past 400 years or in the past 4,000 years, except to the dogmatic Marxist. However, in environmental terms this argument becomes vitally important as will be explained in chapters 3–4. As Chaudhuri argues: "The ceaseless quest of the modern historians looking for the 'origins' and roots of capitalism is not much better than the alchemist's search for the philosopher's stone that transforms base metal into gold" (1990: 84; quoted in Gills, 2000: 2).

These debates on the origins of capitalism and on whether modern capitalism is unique and therefore the only type of capitalism are inherently dependent on how capitalism is defined. It is evident that modern capitalism has various characteristics that distinguish it from previous forms of capitalism but this does not mean that capitalist forms of accumulation did not exist before the seventeenth century (Frank, 1998; Gills, 2000). Modern capitalism does have a specific mode of production that is based on different social relations than previous forms of capitalism. However, this does not mean that embryonic forms of modern capitalist production structures could not be found in previous periods of history.

For the study of the global political economy, it is not necessarily crucial to pin down the exact beginnings of this process and it could be argued that it is impossible to do so. Thus, if globalization is defined as a process that is qualitatively different from previous forms of economic organization and builds upon these, it is not essential to know whether the basis for globalization is modern capitalism or a previous form of capitalism.

Where this debate does become important though is when it comes to the study of particular social and environmental problems associated with globalization and this is why the concept of globalization and historical dimensions are given such prominence here. In order to study these problems and to find solutions to them, it is necessary to be clear about the social and structural origins of these problems. So, for example, it will be crucial to know whether global environmental degradation finds its origins in the mode of production or in the mode of accumulation associated with capitalism (Chew, 2001; Hornborg, 1998). Such evidence will give vital pointers to the origins and sources of environmental degradation and thus substantially advance both the studies of global political economy and also global environmental politics. However, it is very difficult to impossible to find reliable historical data on the phenomenon of environmental degradation under various forms of capitalism. The world systems sociologists have shown that environmental degradation existed in earlier forms of capitalism and can therefore be linked to capitalist modes of accumulation rather than to the modern mode of production (Chew, 2001; Hornborg, 1998, Wallerstein, 1999). However, most social science environmental researchers would argue that there are fundamental differences between fairly localized forms of pollution as found in antiquity and the all-pervasive global degradation found under the fossil fuel economy associated with modern capitalism.

Having flagged some of the definitional problems of the contemporary globalization quagmire, I will now discuss the main approaches to the study of globalization, and global political economy in general, and their ecological dimensions or lack thereof. This overview will highlight the shortcomings of the major approaches to GPE and globalization as well as to their environmental potential. It will also lay the groundwork for the main argument of the book by showing the significance of the three concepts around which the book is organized: historical significance and environment-society relations, production/consumption, and equity.

HISTORICAL APPROACHES

In this category I have grouped together various approaches that take a historical interest in global political economy, notably historical materialist approaches. Here, the work of Cox and of world systems theorists will receive extended attention as they are particularly influential. Unlike many other approaches in IR—such as realism or neoliberal institutionalism—which study the world in the here and now as they find it, historical approaches argue that in order to understand a phenomenon you need to know its social and structural origins and place it in its social context.

Historical materialist positions do this by arguing that political economy and society are fundamentally driven by the social relations of production and that production is the most important factor in historical or contemporary analysis. As Robert Cox states:

> Production creates the material basis for all forms of social existence, and the ways in which human efforts are combined in production processes affect all other aspects of social life, including the polity. Production generates the capacity to exercise power, but power determines the manner in which production takes place (1987: 1).

Cox, being a critical historical materialist and influenced by Antonio Gramsci and Max Weber, actually does not travel down the economic determinist road as far with his statement as other historical materialists. For Cox and followers of this school of thought, changing social relations of production are a major factor in the understanding of progress and of changing economic and political forms of organization. Such economic changes then have an effect on political and social organization. Although it can be argued that the sole emphasis on production as the major agent of change is exaggerated and distorting, it is nevertheless undeniable that the production structure is one of the most salient phenomena of the international or global system. Through the emphasis on the mutual constitution of structure and agency, it is possible to study change over time and not to reduce history to the political wrangling of statespeople. Thus historical materialist approaches, be they Marxist, neo-Gramscian, critical, etc., have a lot to offer to the study of global political economy and they provide a convincing argument for the current globalizing process as a new era by studying the social relations of production over time. However, a narrow emphasis on production also creates major problems. Therefore it is pertinent not to overemphasize historical *materialism* but also to remember the importance of culture, ideology; and philosophy, as the neo-Gramscians themselves argue. The ability to coordinate structure, agency, and social relations are important points for the usefulness of historical materialism as an analytical framework. However, there are also major shortcomings from an eco-holistic perspective. One is the narrow definition of capitalism as a purely modern phenonmenon of this school of thought. Interesting alternatives can be found in the world systems approaches. These will be briefly considered in the next section.

World system analysis sees history divided into certain eras, or systems. Immanuel Wallerstein is the main social architect behind this theory and he places the beginning of the modern capitalist world system at about 1450 and divides it into several periods (1986). However, not all world systems theorists follow this categorization. Both Barry Gills and Andre Gunder Frank provide alternative views (Gills, 2000; Frank, 1998). As Immanuel Wallerstein's categorization is well-known and has been widely discussed, I will concentrate here on Gills's and Frank's account. The main difference between the Wallersteinian and the Gills and Frank argument is a different interpretation of the notion of 'ceaseless accumulation' that Wallerstein dates as beginning around 1450 while Gills and Frank see it as a constant feature of the world system or world economic history (Gills, 2000: 2). The relevance of this argument to the globalization debate and indeed on any debate on the beginnings of capitalism is of course whether capitalism is a fundamentally unique form of social organization of modernity or whether it is something intrinsic in economic and thus in social relations. Frank's and Gills's argument, but intrinsically also Wallerstein's conceptualization, seem to suggest that capitalism per se is continuous in history—although Wallerstein makes a clear distinction between modern and other forms of capitalism. This, then, would suggest that the globalization process is not a unique stage in world history but the natural extension of age-old processes of efficient capital accumulation. However, at the same time it is not the temporary culmination of a linear process because

> There was not one 'feudalisation' but many, not one 'capitalisation' but several, successive waves or high points; not one 'historical capitalism' but many, ancient, medieval and modern as well as Oriental and Occidental. This radical departure from conventional Eurocentric wisdom on world history is the beginning of the necessary re-writing of the social history of capital, of power and of humanity as a whole. It is a new world history (Gills, 2000: 21).

What Gills, and Frank, in contrast to Wallerstein, offer is a new vision of cyclical rather than linear development under differing social conditions and different constellations in social relations. Therefore modern capitalism has its own unique constellations but it still has fundamentally the same basic features of other types of capitalism in history. The same would apply to the globalization process. Although globalization has particular social relations, the fundamental underlying principles of its economic organization are still the same as other types of capitalism. For example, post-Fordism is different from Fordism or from previous labor relations but it is still a form of labor relations that is geared toward the most efficient production structure of the particular social context in terms of social relations and state of technological progress. Therefore globalization can be seen as a continuous social process that has accelerated its speed over the past thirty years or so rather than a completely new form of socio-economic organization.

Historical approaches to global political economy and to globalization primarily focus on the explanation of how this globalizing phenomenon or process came about and they do this from a historical materialist perspective. The nature and evolution of capitalism is a primary factor in this explanatory endeavor. There are conflicting interpretations of the nature and origins of capitalism with traditional approaches seeing modern capitalism as a unique form of economic organization while the world systems theory of Gills and Frank suggests that capitalism is an ever-present phenomenon of history and that modern capitalism may be qualitatively different from previous forms but they are still all capitalism. While the first view takes a linear view of history, world systems theory (as opposed to world-systems theory) takes a combined linear-cyclical view of history. One approach sees the evolution of the global political economy as a new form of previously existing capitalism that is not fundamentally different from previous experiences while the other approach sees it as a new stage of capitalism in a linear progression. Neither approach has a prescriptive component, whether analytically or morally motivated.

There are two aspects missing from these existing historical perspectives: on the one hand they focus almost exclusively on the production structure as the primary engine of history to the exclusion of environmental and other contextual factors. The history of nature-society relations and their effects on the evolution of capitalism is of vital importance but has been excluded from analysis. On the other hand, other economic agents in the economic structure have also been neglected. Production structure does not equal economic structure and a wider angle is needed.

Although historical materialist approaches do not have an environmental dimension per se, there is a body of literature on the subject of environment and capitalism that will be discussed in detail in chapter 3 (Lipschutz 2001a, 1993; Paterson, 2000; Chew, 2001; Hornborg, 1998; Wallerstein, 1999). This literature is primarily concerned with either the relationship between nature and society (not necessarily in a global but in a general context) or specific case studies within the global political economy (Paterson, 1996). Thus a large-scale integration of environmental thought into historical materialist thought has so far not taken place although the conceptual capacity is clearly there. It would necessitate a move away from economic determinism toward a recognition that not only production but also 'nature's larder' provide the 'material basis for all forms of social existence,' to borrow Cox's phrase (1987: 1). In short, a theoretical readjustment is necessary that acknowledges a connection between the primacy of the production structure and a dependency on a finite ecosystem for this production structure to be sustained. Nevertheless, the historical materialist school of thought is the most promising starting point for a marriage between ecological thought and global political economy and such an endeavor will thus be pursued in more depth in this book.

THE LIBERAL APPROACH

The liberal approach is one that can be evenly divided into a conceptual and a policy-related approach as it is the hegemonic approach of not only global environmental politics but also of the global political economy architecture in general. The classic IPE textbooks define liberal IPE in the following three ways:

> Liberal economic theory is committed to free markets and minimal state intervention, although the relative emphasis on the one or the other may differ. Liberal political theory is committed to individual equality and liberty, although again the emphasis may differ (Gilpin, 1987: 27).

> Whereas the realist approach focuses on the nation-state, liberal thinking has tended to see the individual as the basic unit of analysis. The primary motivating force in the economy is the competitive interaction between individuals, who are assumed to maximize their satisfaction, or utility, especially through the social institution of the market. The market aggregates these individual preferences and utilities (on the demand side) and (on the supply side) the actions of profit-seeking firms. Some modern liberal thinkers, notably von Hayek, have argued that the market is, in fact, a spontaneous social institution, rather than an institution which is a product of human design (Stephen Gill & David Law, 1988: 42).

> Liberalism is a view of IPE that sees markets as more important than states. The role of the market is as a peaceful coordinating process, which brings together individuals in a mutually advantageous positive-sum game. The role of state power is negligible, largely confined to security structures, or stronger, but mainly used to strengthen and stabilize markets. In any case, the market is seen as the driving force of IPE and state power is generally suspect and must be justified to appeal to reason (Balaam & Veseth, 1996: 56).

Despite their differences, all approaches make it clear that liberal IPE is about the importance of the economy and access to markets, i.e. advocating free markets. The benefits of free markets will also accrue in the political field through increased wealth for all and more economic interdependence will lead to less conflict. These ideas and principles have been anchored in a global political economy framework through the Bretton Woods system and through the creation of organizations designed to increase economic integration between the various parts of the world.

International economic integration institutions such as the World Bank, the International Monetary Fund, the World Trade Organisation, and regional economic integration organizations have especially changed the political and economic landscape from the 1970s onward. Most of these institutions have of course existed since the end of the Second World War and were architects of the post-war political and economic order. With the collapse of the original Bretton Woods system in the 1970s and the ensuing changes in the production structure, these institutions have also gradually experienced a change in the international economic order to which they have contributed.

The field of trade is perhaps the area in which most of the change has taken place. Although there have been historical periods of trade liberalization before, notably in the nineteenth century, and this new era of moving toward freer trade is not unprecedented (Schwartz, 2000; Hirst & Thompson, 1996), the degree of institutionalization of the present trade liberalization era is quite unprecedented. The General Agreement on Tariffs and Trade served as the international organization responsible for trade liberalization until 1994 when it was replaced with the World Trade Organisation. The World Trade Organisation is perceived as one of the main culprits of the negative effects of economic globalization by the general public, largely because of the attention it has received from protest movements. Both the GATT and the WTO have changed the landscape of international trade. Although this is a process that is not related to the collapse of the Bretton Woods system but to the design of the international post-war order, it nevertheless accelerated in the later decades of the twentieth century. Trade liberalization was discussed in trade rounds dealing with specific products and product groups. However, this was primarily a trend affecting goods produced by industrialized countries and most trade liberalization took place within the industrialized world.

Apart from being a legally stronger and more wide-reaching organization compared to the GATT, the WTO

> aims to reduce or eliminate a whole range of non-tariff barriers and differences in trading conditions between countries. Moreover, the WTO is a much more powerful institution in so far as its dispute panels have the authority to make binding judgements in cases where trade rules are subject to dispute or transgressed (Held et al., 1999: 165).

The reduction of non-tariff barriers is one of the fields where the WTO has been severely criticized because many of these barriers are in place to protect certain social and human rights or environmental standards that then have to be eroded or subordinated to WTO/GATT rules. Therefore the harmonization of import and export rules to liberalize trade has an impact on other policy areas or social issues. The present arrangement whereby WTO rules can, and usually do, take precedence over international environmental agreements or national regulations, for example, may not directly affect state sovereignty as a legal issue but at the same time it erodes the power of the state to be in control of its social and environmental regulations if it wants to be part of the global economic framework. This is a problem that affects both industrialized and developing countries. Thus one of the main criticisms of the World Trade Organisation and of economic globalization (the term used to describe neoliberal policy aims) is that the increasing importance of markets erodes the power of states and gives power to non-elected economic organizations such as multinational corporations (Hines, 2000). States then become more interested in supporting their economies rather than their citizens, arguing that a well-functioning economy is good for their citizens. The state thus becomes a representative of the economic actors rather than social interests, marginalizing citizens and reducing them to economic actors rather than to private citizens.

One of the main problems with this construction is that it leads to an institutional network prioritizing free markets or trade liberalization over most or all other policy issues, automatically assuming that such trends are beneficial for society at large. However, such a view ignores the fact that there are certain policy areas that cannot easily be accommodated in an economo-centric worldview and that this leads to a lack of moral agency in the international system. The protection of minimum labor standards and basic human rights for workers or the protection of the environment are a case in point. If increasing trade liberalization and erosion of non-tariff barriers makes it difficult for individual states to introduce or uphold production, labor, or environmental standards because they would constitute an unfair obstacle to fair trade, then the agency of the World Trade Organisation clearly has a globalizing effect in terms of introducing a liberated market. However, it also introduces a level playing field at the level of the lowest common denominator in terms of labor, environmental and production standards and makes it difficult for states with low denominators to rise above that situation. In order to participate in the global market, states are compelled to comply with the rules set up by the WTO. This affects or erodes their sovereign right to self-determination in terms of national legislation.

Legally, this right to sovereignty is not affected but it is impeded in practice as the whole global economic integration project makes it impossible for a state to 'opt out'. Not all academics or policy makers agree that trade liberalization leads to lower social or environmental standards. Daniel Drezner (2001), for example, argues that trade liberalization and economic institutionalization through the WTO has actually led to higher labor or environmental standards in developing countries. The discrepancies between these arguments may well be specific to economic sectors or related to measurement of improvement. Drezner measures improvement in terms of legislation or regulations whereas critics tend to look at living and working conditions as well as at the structural framework. It is also necessary to make distinctions between absolute and relative improvements. Liberals believe that absolute gains are an improvement while critics of this approach, such as historical materialists, hold that an absolute improvement of a situation may well (and usually does) mean a relative worsening of a particular state's or region's position in the world economy—either in terms of economic performance or in terms of welfare or environmental standards. In fact, world gross product has more than quadrupled since 1950 (New Scientist, April 27, 2002: 31) yet at the same time the gap between rich and poor has increased tenfold (ibid.). Thus, despite the fact that absolute wealth has increased on the planet (e.g., witnessed by a steadily declining infant mortality rate), inequality on the planet has actually increased because wealth in developed countries has increased to such an exponential extent.

The idea of global trade liberalization is a value-neutral project that is based on classical liberal ideas of increased overall wealth benefiting everybody in the long run. However, this point of view disregards the actual nature of capital accumulation and its profit motive that is disconnected from moral and ethical considerations. As long as there are expanding markets, moral and ethical considerations toward the work force need not be considered as they are not seen as potential consumers of the product. Likewise, environmental responsibility is externalized and cannot be reconciled with a profit motive. Therefore a moral authority needs to represent the 'common good' and so far this role has been taken over by the state (Altvater & Mahnkopf, 1999; Bauman, 1998a, b). As this role of the state has now been curtailed through the primacy of the market over welfare agendas, this creates serious problems in terms of moral authority in the international system. However, states themselves have been complicit in this process and relegated themselves to a lower place on the international agenda. Therefore, in terms of agency the WTO cannot be held responsible for this process as it has been set up by an international community of states in order to do exactly what it does—to liberalize trade (Kreissl-Dörfler, 1997).

Another group of actors supposedly complicit in the construction of a global economy are multinational corporations—the very actors who are meant to benefit most from trade liberalization. Sheer size and economic impact gives many of the larger companies a disproportionate influence in certain geographical regions. It has been argued that some multinational corporations use this power to extract concessions from governments/states by uttering threats of relocation or demand subsidies for setting up business in a certain geographical area. This is a problem faced by both developing and developed countries (Strange, 1996). However, other sources maintain that the actual occurrence and empirical evidence for such behavior is rather more scant than globalization critics would make us believe (Drezner, 2001). Therefore this claim is contested. It cannot be denied that the profit and efficiency rationale of big business in the era of post-Fordism leads to global practices that contribute to the erosion of human and labor rights as well as to environmental degradation, but this sort of behavior seems to be guided by functionality rather than by a plot to assume power in world politics. These negative effects seem to be unintended consequences as they are outside the framework within which policy is made.

However, this view is not shared by many of the new social movements that have developed the mission to demonstrate and fight against the negative effects of economic globalization. These actors are non-governmental organizations (NGOs) but also more informally organized groupings that have come together to stop the downward spiral of environmental and social degradation (Keck & Sikkink, 1998; Lipschutz, 1996). They are actors who benefit from political liberalism and are a counterforce to the negative impact of neoliberal economic policy. Although these are organizations with no clear legal or legitimate mandate to act in the international system, they find strong public support and have often been invited to participate in international policy-making on an informal and advisory basis. Although NGOs participated in the global political process long before 1992, the precedent for large-scale NGO and social movement involvement in international affairs was set at the 1992 Rio Summit and has since become commonplace in international environmental policy-making. The World Bank, too, has started cooperation with non-governmental organizations but the WTO and the IMF have no such sophisticated coordinated consultation mechanisms in place (yet)—or at least not to such an extent. To be sure, the WTO consults with business NGOs but as a rule not with social and environmental NGOs. So there is a gradual change happening in the international system with more actors evolving who want to leave their imprint on the policy-making process. However, in terms of NGO/new social movement involvement this is a voluntary process and these actors have no official legal role in international decision-making. In many ways their legitimacy as international actors in such processes could also be questioned as these are not democratically elected institutions with a clearly defined mandate (Jordan & Maloney, 1996). However, it is recognized that these organizations represent parts of society and public opinion and are therefore an important addition to the policy process.

These developments show that the liberal and neoliberal approaches to globalization are very much the hegemonic approach to the global political economy as they are so much embedded in actual practice and value structure of the global institutional architecture. But where does that leave the environment? Liberal approaches have a strong environmental component but this is related to wealth creation. For example, the Brundtland report (1987) equates poverty with environmental degradation and sees the solution to environmental problems in the increase of wealth within a society, which will then give society the financial means to put regulatory structures in place. Of course this approach denies the essential link between environmental degradation and wealth creation since it is excessive consumption and use of resources and degrading sinks, i.e., using ecosystems to deposit the wastes of the industrial production process that causes most environmental degradation. Thus liberalism and an advanced economic society create the financial resources necessary to manage environmental problems generated by its excessive wealth generation. Liberal IPE or (global political economy) GPE sees the environment as a problem of financial input and management rather than as a problem of resource use and distribution (Young, 1997; Bernstein, 2001; Stevis & Assetto, 2001). Thus liberalism sees environmental degradation as an economic problem rather than as a problem of the interdependence of industrial society and the environment in which it exists and on which it is dependent. Therefore, I argue that although there is copious literature on environmental regimes, environmental management, and liberal environmentalism, this does not constitute a liberal theory of the environment, even less so a liberal theory of environmental IPE. To achieve such a theory, liberalism would need to rethink the relations between environment and society in a fundamental way that does not see the environment as merely an economic input problem.

These are in direct juxtaposition to the views of most liberals, both on issues such as justice and economic globalization and the environment.

THE GLOBALIZATION CRITICS

This section is focused on the voluminous and sometimes populist literature that sees globalization as a force to be resisted. This literature sees globalization as the consequence of neoliberal institutions and policies that find their origins in the political and economic framework set up after the Second World War.

Ankie Hoogvelt defines neoliberalism in the following way:

> At the heart of this 'neoliberal' ideology is the idea that private property and accumulation are sacrosanct and that the prime responsibility of governments is to ensure 'sound finance': they must 'fight inflation' and maintain an attractive 'business climate' in which, amongst other things, the power of unions is circumscribed. These ideas both underpin and are the result of the 'structural power' of

> capital that is so internationally mobile that the investment climate
> of each country is continually judged by business with reference to
> the climate which prevails elsewhere (1997: 135).

The protection and importance of private property is a classic tenant of liberal thought and its emphasis as such is nothing particularly new and unique to the process of globalization. However, its overemphasis is the main characteristic of neoliberal globalization and so is the subordination of other liberal principles to this idea. The changing role of the state in the global economy is a primary factor in the rise of neoliberalism. Internationalization of production in itself is nothing new and is a permanent feature of most forms of capitalism. States were the accepted guardians of domestic concerns such as welfare and employment and economic progress. The prevailing liberal ideology was supportive of trade liberalization and of the international movement of capital but states were seen as the main agents in this process; hence the liberalism of this form of capitalism was called embedded as it was incorporated into national structures (Ruggie, 1982; Gill & Mittelman, 1997). The main difference between liberalism and neoliberalism is that under the process of globalization economic structures are disembedded and the responsibilities of the state shift from protecting citizens and other agents to strengthening its place in a competitive world economy, thereby giving its citizens the protection previously enjoyed in different forms. Thus the state has become the guardian of capital and production only rather than labor, welfare, or particular industries. The rise of multilateral institutions and new social movements within this process have attracted a lot of attention and have been documented in detail elsewhere (O'Brien et al., 2000).

In this approach, the World Trade Organization is seen as the most obvious manifestation of neoliberalism and of the erosion of the power of the state. Its establishment in 1995 gave it more legal clout and institutional status than the GATT. As Colin Hines puts it:

> The WTO's greatest power lies in its dispute settlement body and
> its cross-retaliation provisions, both of which enable it to force
> nations to comply with WTO rules. The increasing number of
> controversial rulings in which the WTO dispute settlement body
> has upheld corporate interests over those of people and the environment has increased public opposition to the WTO. . . . Globalization is reducing the power of governments to provide what their
> populations require all over the world. TNCs and international
> capital have become the *de facto* new world government. Their
> increasing control over the global economy is underpinned by their
> free trade orthodoxy (2000: 16).

The advent of the WTO parallels in the economic sphere the institutionalization found in the political sphere for the past fifty years. The United Nations system and the International Court of Justice have similarly institutionalized procedures for interstate relations in all sorts of spheres and have provided a dispute-settlement body in the form of the International Court of Justice in The Hague. The statement that the WTO has more power than states is dependent on the definition of power used. The concept of state sovereignty has not changed and states are still the only sovereign actors in the international system. Just as with the International Court of Justice where there is no enforcement mechanism for the legally binding decisions of the Court, the dispute settlement body of the WTO may be legally binding but there is no enforcement mechanism apart from trade sanctions. These trade sanctions may be very harmful and be a de facto limitation of state sovereignty but in legal terms the WTO is not more powerful than states. So the actual influence of international economic actors may have increased over time under the process of globalization but the actual status of states has not changed, or rather the effects of neoliberalism have not fundamentally altered the institutional structure of the international system.

In the environmental literature, such discourses have been approached through the conceptualization of non-state actors. The popular global civil society discourse has become prominent within critical and alternative GPE. It is mainly concerned with the rise of global environmental movements as significant actors in the international system who are able to shape global and local agendas (Lipschutz, 1996; Keck & Sikkink, 1998; Conca, 2001). A recent example of this are the protests at the 1999 World Trade Organisation Summit meeting in Seattle or the 2001 G8 summit of the world's seven leading economic powers plus Russia in Genoa. Therefore this body of literature is mainly concerned with the role of agency in the global system and how agency has been transformed under conditions of globalization, such as the rise of more transnational actors in the international system and the perceived erosion of state sovereignty or the change in the role of the state in general.

Although it is certainly true that the role or level of activity of global civil society has either increased dramatically in the past twenty years or has become more visible, these developments have given many non-state actors a more prominent role in the international system as policy advisers and conference participants. However, in legal terms the role of the state has not changed in this period and nor have international organizations fundamentally changed their organizational structures. The Rio Summit in 1992 created a precedent by giving many non-state actors a prominent position in agenda-setting processes and debates but these actors have not acquired decision-making powers and have remained consultation partners rather than equal actors. So, although these new social movements are widespread in the global environmental field, they are not an environmental phenomenon as such as they can equally be found in other policy areas. Therefore the global civil society literature uses the environment as a case study for its approach rather than offering an environmental perspective for the globalization debate.

Some writers see these new social movements or global civil society as the main avenue through which political and economic change toward a more sustainable political economy can be enacted given their belief that the rigidity of institutional frameworks prevents effective policy options from reaching this side (Wapner, 1998; Bryner, 2001). Thus an argument for the particularly environmental nature of this approach can be made. The actual role of global civil society in bringing about environmental improvement or economic change will be discussed in chapters 4–6 and the weight of this argument assessed.

Another point of departure in the globalization critics' account of the process of globalization is the increased power that multinational corporations seem to enjoy. This is seen as a particularly worrying phenomenon because it affects the issue of legitimacy in the international system. Multinational corporations are primarily accountable to their shareholders and their profit motive is thus to ensure high ratings on the stock market and high dividends to shareholders. This means that their investment policies are very short-term and that economies of flexibility and efficiency are at the forefront of decision-making strategies rather than the long-term interests of the company. In addition, companies as economic actors are profit-oriented and do not have a social or public responsibility toward people or toward the environment, a role traditionally carried out by governments. Therefore the increased clout of multinational corporations at the expense of the state means that such social responsibilities are neglected. The idea that the market as the primary forum of international relations incorporates social responsibilities and the fulfillment of basic needs of the weak is questioned by the globalization critics (Thomas, 2000, Hines, 2000).

The reason why multinational corporations are doing well in a globalizing economic climate is because trade liberalization and economies of flexibility and free flow of capital benefit the ones who already have capital and a large share in international trade (Thomas, 2000). In this situation existing comparative advantages in the international economic system can be used to further extend the position of multinational corporations to one of dominance in the market. Because they contribute such a large proportion of gross national product (GNP), employment figures, corporate taxes, etc. these corporations are able to influence governments and regional integration organizations to represent their interests as it will be to everybody's benefit that the multinational corporations are doing well. However, the strong criticisms faced by these corporations from the globalization critics and the simultaneous decline of the state can also be seen as exaggerated phenomena. As Herman Schwartz argues:

> Just as states consciously created markets in the first place from 1500 through 1914, states have consciously recreated markets today. From 1500 to around 1800 those states made markets in agricultural goods and tried to extend those markets into all agricultural production. In the long 19th century they made markets in industrial goods and this finally did facilitate the extension of markets into agriculture with disastrous results in the 1930s. Today states are making markets in the service sectors which they had regulated and sheltered from the market since the Depression. As in the 19th century, the re-emergence of markets was planned by market actors and states that stood to benefit from the destruction or reconfiguration of the various forms of social protection created in the 'golden era' of the Keynesian welfare state. . . . But the driving force (behind globalization) is still conflict between states worried about global market shares, states reacting to shifts in their relative ability to generate export streams and attract capital investment (2000: 318).

What Schwartz is saying is that multinational corporations have not taken power away from the state but have colluded and cooperated with states to bring about the free market ideology of neoliberalism under which globalization is thriving. This argument is also valid in the context of the WTO since the WTO was set up by and for states and the changes in the political economy that led to the beginning of the globalization process were also enacted by states. So on the one hand there is an erosion of the power of the state but on the other the new system benefits those states that were in a powerful situation when the system was established and therefore strengthens their position in the international system. Thus some of the arguments of the globalization critics are overly simplistic although the fundamental critique that the conditions under globalization are becoming less socially aware and more individualistic are certainly true. Although institutions such as the World Trade Organisation or regional economic integration organizations certainly do seem to erode the power of the state and place more emphasis on free markets, economic growth, and progress rather than on human welfare, the state, or rather the developed world, have been instrumental in bringing about this new institutional framework and are playing a central role in it. The state has not been coerced into changing its role.

CONCLUSION

This chapter has critically examined the concept and processes of a globalizing political economy in relation to theory and policy practice as well as relating to environmental and social concerns. Globalization both as a concept and as a process is a contested term—its usage has become generally accepted but there is no definition of what constitutes globalization and there is no empirical evidence that it exists on a large scale. Attempts to conceptualize or theorize about globalization from an IPE perspective tend to sideline the environmental and social consequences of globalization as issues in the intellectual framework within which globalization is analyzed. These issues are usually treated as part of an analysis of global civil society and new social movements but in this context only transnational actors representing social and environmental issues are incorporated into the analysis rather than the structural and systemic forces and constraints within which actors operate. There is a shortage of literature on this subject and this book aims to address this gap in the literature by offering a conceptual analysis of the social relations between the various actors in the global system and the structural environment in which they operate.

The reason why there is no specifically environmental theory of GPE is that the social sciences do not generally theorize about the environment as they are primarily concerned with society. The environment enters social science either as a problem to be solved by society, a force dominating society, a force to be dominated by society, or in the form of nature-society relations. It is the latter concept that is relevant as a theoretical concept for GPE.

The term eco-holistic is a new concept, denoting the need to merge the concerns of both holistic and ecocentric approaches. Holistic approaches have traditionally been focused on traditional social science, incorporating social, political, and economic factors but have not usually included environmental criteria. Ecocentric approaches, on the other hand, focus on the ecological aspect of analysis, thus usually subordinating the social, political and economic angle. The term 'eco-holistic' emphasizes that analysis needs to be social, political, economic, *and* environmental. This chapter has subjected the core global political economy approaches to a preliminary eco-holistic analysis. Chapters 2–4 of this conceptual part of this book will argue the case for three main pillars around which an eco-holistic GPE should be based, namely the historical dimension of environment-society relations, the production/consumption debate, and equity.

Chapter 2

Linking Environment and Society

This chapter will investigate the role between environment and society in the globalizing political economy as well as the social and structural origins of environmental degradation. This subject has not previously been researched as such. There are many studies on the various actors in environmental politics and some studies on environmental ideologies (Laferrière and Stoett, 1999; Peet and Watts, 1996; Escobar, 1996) as well as studies on the commodification of the environment under modern capitalism (Merchant, 1992). However, there has not been any systematic research in International Relations (IR) or in any other discipline on the changing relations between society and environment throughout history and the underlying structural forces leading to these changes, which would be crucial for an understanding of the relationship between globalization and environmental degradation. This chapter is an attempt to remedy this shortcoming and sees this task as the first step toward an environmental or eco-holistic global political economy approach.

Traditionally, literature focusing on the relationship between nature or environment and society or culture has taken the rise of modern capitalism with the associated rises of enlightenment thinking, Newtonian science, and the industrial revolution as the starting point of disturbed nature-society relations. This view tends to romanticize the environmental impact of pre-industrial society, or as Luc Ferry puts it, in a different context, 'it is possible to denounce the real or imagined misdeeds of liberalism in the name of nostalgia' (1995: xxvi). There have been several studies (Ponting, 1991; Chew, 2001) that have demonstrated that pre-industrial or pre-modern capitalist societies also engaged in practices resulting in widespread environmental degradation. However, it is often argued, that these degrading practices had a local or regional rather than global impact and that modern capitalism and its social relations are the only forms of social organization that actually lead to *global* environmental degradation. Not all pollution in modernity is global pollution but modernity is the only form of social organization that can produce global pollution due to its global structures. This argument will be investigated further in this chapter because it is vitally important to establish whether the actual structures of modern capitalism intrinsically lead to more global environmental degradation compared with earlier forms of capitalism or if the increasing global nature of pollution can actually be attributed to technological progress rather than to underlying structural forces. This question is crucial for finding the right way to approach the environmental crisis going beyond a purely management-based approach.

The global nature of environmental degradation can largely be linked to the rise of the fossil fuel economy and to the decreasing distance of time and space in the relations between different parts of the globe (Daly, 1996). These phenomena are intrinsically linked to the rise of modern capitalism. However, the latter point is part of a longer and larger process that can also be observed in pre-modernity. The first section of this chapter will be concerned with exploring this point in detail and discussing the historical origins of contemporary nature and society relations.

The chapter will then investigate the particular relationship of environment and society under the process of globalization. Here, several phenomena will be studied in detail as they are seen as vital ingredients of this process. The understanding of time as a social and environmental phenomenon will be a primary focus of this investigation. This point will be extended to focus on the phenomenon of time-space distanciation, which is often cited as one of the primary phenomena of globalization as it is generally associated with the globalizing of production and communication. However, it is even more pertinent in relation to the spread and structural origins of environmental degradation. These issues highlight the historical dimension of environment-society relations around which this chapter is centered.

Another globalizing field is the study of governance and the increasing number of global accords regulating the social and economic activities that lead to environmental degradation. These agreements tend to be de-linked from the relationship between environment and society and focus on environmental management strategies and damage-limitation exercises rather than dealing with the structural roots of particular environmental problems.

In this context, the subject of trade and the environment also needs to be examined given that global trade regimes promote an unsustainable trading pattern that goes against the grain of resource realities. Trade and the environment are issues that have been linked in the academic literature but in practice trade liberalization and environmental protection are unrelated concepts and environmental considerations are only given lip service in the institutionalization of trade. The latter issues of governance and trade are seen as threads that will go through all of the three main concepts I have signposted as the main pillars of an eco-holistic global political economy—environment-society relations, production-consumption, and equity.

LINKING ENVIRONMENT AND POLITICAL ECONOMY

Traditionally, political economy analysis in IR goes back to the beginnings of modern capitalism and to the social relations that evolve in this period and then develop and change throughout modernity (Fox, 1998; Gill & Mittelman, 1997; Hoogvelt, 1997). The environment has not formed part of this analysis although it has entered the field through radical/political/historical ecology and types of ecological economics analysis (Merchant, 1992; Daly, 1996; Eckersley, 1995; Dryzek, 1997). These approaches usually define the rise of modern capitalism as the point in history where society became more alienated from its physical environment than it used to be, a process that became worse as modern capitalism became more sophisticated. Basically, the rise of modern capitalism, enlightenment, Newtonian science, and the industrial revolution acted in concert to bring about a change in society-environment relations as humans in the core economies saw themselves as increasingly mastering nature rather than being dependent and dominated by it (Merchant, 1992). This in turn led to the perceived notion of decreasing dependency on the environment that resulted in its neglect through lack of understanding of ecological processes and their significance for life on the planet.

This view of environmental political economy is a fundamentally Eurocentric but also technological/economic determinist view of history. First of all, the notion of the mastering of nature is confined to the industrializing countries and not a global phenomenon. Even today, nature-society relations are far from universal and can take different forms and shapes in different infrastructures even within the same national society. For example, in an advanced industrial society, people have a relationship with their immediate local environment if they live in rural areas or a relationship with the countryside as visited at weekends or during holidays for city dwellers. They also have a relationship with the physical environment as experienced while traveling and they have images of what nature is and what its role should be in modern life. This is their immediately experienced relationship and differs fundamentally from the environment-society relations of a predominantly agricultural developing country such as flood-ridden Mozambique. Therefore it is misleading to speak of 'the' environment-society relationship as there are many different such relations in different societies or different segments of society. Likewise, different nature-society relations are experienced in different aspects of people's lives.

However, nature-society relations that are not consciously experienced are much more significant in political economy terms. These are experienced through productive and consumptive relations but the ecological or environmental aspects of these are not perceived by the various actors in the international system, or domestic systems, and their side effects in terms of environmental degradation are de-contextualized through the separation of environmental from other types of policy. What this means is that social behavior and actions have a much larger impact on the environment through the environmental impact of economic activities far removed from the actual consumer and that these practices are vitally important in shaping environment-society relations. However, these relations are usually not analyzed in the type of context suggested here.

Because of the complexity of environment-society relations at the conscious and subconscious levels as well as at the local, regional, and global level it is difficult to integrate this into a global political economy of the environment. However, because of this diversity of relations, it is also difficult to make a case for fundamentally changed nature-society relations after the industrial revolution and the beginning of modern capitalism from a global perspective. Therefore a theory based on the assumption that there is one environment-society relationship and that this relationship is fundamentally different from the pre-modernity relationship is reductionist and cannot be the basis of a consistent political economy of the environment.

An alternative to this view is the ecological world systems theory approach (Hornborg, 1998; Chew, 1998, 2001; Goldfrank, Goodman, & Szasz, 1999). The main argumentative thrust of this type of analysis suggests that the rise and fall of world civilizations can be traced to environmental degradation. Thus, the nature of capitalism can be understood through the social relations of production, labor, and the environment. Clive Ponting (1991) in his environmental history of the world advances a similar argument, however, not couched in theoretical terms. These are views of history that integrate an environmental or ecological perspective into predominantly social historical accounts. They are also views that include an account of environment-society relations as connections are made between productive and consumptive relations and economic performance as well as the negative impact of environmental degradation on economic performance. So from this point of view an ecological world systems approach can offer an interesting alternative to the historical materialist orthodoxy that points out the connection between fundamentally changed society-environment relations and the rise of modern capitalism.

The main argument of Sing Chew's thesis, for example, is that different phases in world history and the rise and fall of trading relations can be analyzed from a historical materialist perspective as done by Wallerstein or alternatively, by Frank and Gills, and focus on the social relations of production. However, these approaches neglect the relationship between nature/natural resources and the material basis of production. In fact, the demise of most empires or large powers also coincides with a decline in the natural resource base through overexploitation or through other exhaustion. In fact, forensic research suggests that even the two historical periods of dark ages are linked to the depletion of the natural resource base and this has been documented in carbon testing from these areas (Chew, 2001). So, for example, the dark ages in Germany and Sweden are accompanied by a decline in forestation and the local economies started to recover once reforestation had taken place. This type of pattern is reproduced over time and over space and a strong argument can be made that environmental degradation is a strong factor in world system formation and decline.

This type of approach integrates the environment into political economy in a holistic manner integrating social with environmental analysis. It also has the potential for a holistic account of environment-society relations. The ecological world systems approach overcomes the difficulties associated with a narrow account of the structural origins of environmental degradation as the result of the rise of modern capitalism. It does not narrowly associate the rise of environmental degradation with a particular mode of production and blames the mode of accumulation, which can be found in all capitalist systems. It therefore offers a much wider definition of capitalism based on accumulation rather than on the specific mode of production found under modern capitalism. However, this argument could then be extended to make a case for traditional forms of capitalism leading to regional and local environmental degradation. The advanced mode of production related to the industrial revolution and the associated predominance and hegemony of the fossil fuel economy, on the other hand, leads to the spreading and globalizing of environmental degradation through its global reach. So, in fact it is not the changing relations of production under modern capitalism that lead to dramatically changed environment-society relations but the technological advances of this period. These are associated with changed notions of progress and speed of change. Environmental degradation has always existed under systems of mass production and modern capitalism is merely a qualitatively different phase of this problem.

The extension of consumption and thus increased demand leading to more efficient production methods and the advances in technology and scientific knowledge are all related to, and constitutive of, the social relations of production and consumption. These social relations led to the vast extension of trade and consumption of resources and to an increasing internationalization and eventual globalization of the forces of production. This inter- and transnationalization and eventual globalization of the political economy also results in an internationalization and globalization of the environmental side effects of this extended production base. This can explain why modern capitalism sees a variety of local, regional, and global environmental degradation and previous forms of economic organization that were limited to local and regional environmental effects. Most global environmental effects can be traced back to the fossil fuel economy, although from a structural point of view, the global structure of production can be indirectly used to make a case for describing local or regional pollution as a global phenomenon.

ENVIRONMENT AND GLOBALIZATION

Having established the historical context in which environment-society relations have evolved and have been analyzed, the cardinal question is whether any aspect of the globalizing of social relations fundamentally alters environment-society relations as compared to pre-globalization forms of economic organization.

The process of globalization is characterized by a globalizing of production processes, a global division of labor, and the liberalization of trade and finance (Mittelman, 1997; Paterson, 2001). Although these changing structures of economic activity obviously draw after themselves environmental effects, it could be argued that these effects are primarily manifested in increased consumption and increased exploitation of resources and sinks as well as the exploration of previously unused resources and sinks. Thus, there is a change in volume of exploitation but not a qualitative or structural change. Such increased consumption and exploitation is not a new process started under globalization but the continuation of an increasing and expanding international and globalizing economy under modern capitalism as such. So from this point of view environment-society relations in the age of globalization are not fundamentally different from previous periods. However, it can be argued that there are important changes in environment-society relations that are not immediately obvious but that are still of vital importance.

These changes can primarily be found in the privatizing of nature/environment through the tenets of neoliberal ideology (Peluso & Watts, 2001; Paterson, 2001). Through the globalizing of production and finance, the regulation of environmental degradation at the local or national level becomes more difficult because the agents of pollution are not usually located near the source of pollution, although their economic activities take place there. At the same time, environment-society relations in the industrialized, consumer countries are not fundamentally changed while the relations between society and environment in developing countries are increasingly shaped by the global or Northern political economy and increasingly less so by local factors (Clapp, 2001). This point applies to both industrializing and primarily agricultural countries. So, in global terms globalization has fundamentally changed environment-society relations although this is not immediately obvious from the vantage point of the Northern citizen.

Although it is true that even under colonialism the colonies' environment-society relations were affected by the colonizer and shaped to fulfill demand in the colonizer's economy, this happened in a structure where the colonizer had an interest in the continued productivity of the land tilled, which implied an incentive of stability. Under globalization, this is not the case. As there is a free or near-free market of resources and sinks, it is possible to exploit these resources without being interested in their continued well functioning (unless they are very scarce) as they can be abandoned for better locations as soon as more efficient production sites elsewhere become available. Since the 'exploiter' does not own the land but only pays to make use of it, there is no long-term interest and responsibility as the risks and responsibilities are externalized.

So in effect globalization can be described as a new ecological imperialism. This point will be developed further in section 2 of this book where it will also be placed in the context of deteriorating social conditions going hand in hand with environmental degradation. What is clear though is that globalization has more fundamental and far-reaching consequences for environment-society relations in developing countries than it has for the Northern Hemisphere that has a long history of having benefited from the exploitation of developing countries, or colonies.

Another aspect of the globalization of the environment is an evolving global consciousness and global ethics among certain groupings in civil society resulting in protests against the neoliberal ideology of economic liberalization, privatization, and lack of public responsibility (J. A. Fox, 1998; Newell, 2001; Lipschutz, 1996; Bryner, 2001). This is seen as a counterhegemonic force against the rise of the multinational corporation and the institutionalization of global economic regimes cementing neoliberal principles. Traditionally, such social movements operated primarily at the national or maybe regional level but recently there has been a proliferation of coalitions and solidarity movements that take on a transnational and an increasingly global character (Keck & Sikkink, 1998; Bryner, 2001). This building of civil society or new social movements is a new phenomenon that can only be compared to the trade union movement that has tended to lose power with the globalizing of production. It is questionable, however, if these new social movements can actually be said to have achieved the status of a counterhegemonic bloc as is often claimed. This phenomenon has received serious attention by the globalization and also by environmental academics and policy makers and will not be pursued further here as it has been analyzed in detail elsewhere.

Rather, this chapter will continue to focus on the more structural aspects of globalization and environment. Loosely following Susan Strange's taxonomy of dividing the world into structures, this chapter will now examine different types of structures that are seen as formative in determining environment-society relations under the process of globalization. These are time and time-space distanciation as the underlying principles according to which local-global linkages are constituted, complemented by the discussion of the liberalization and institutionalization of trade and the topic of global governance.

TIME

Globalization is mostly analyzed in spatial terms or from a historical perspective. I will put forward an alternative form of analysis here based on a juxtaposition of social and ecological time. Such a conceptualization of time is important for the understanding of the evolution of global political economy because it provides an eco-holistic understanding of socio-economic development but also provides a good understanding of environment-society relations. Time is a notoriously difficult concept to define and exists at various levels of differing complexity. Here, I will focus on the relationship between social and ecological time. Social time is generally regarded as a measurement or as a tool for organization. This is fundamentally different from ecological time that is not a social construct but a complicated natural mechanism that has to be conceptualized and harmonized with social time. In social science analysis social time is to be the measurement against which environment is studied. However, since all social constructs are located in a physical environment, it is necessary to embed social analysis in a wider understanding of ecological time.

Both time and the environment are frameworks within which social relations occur: they are part of the social framework but at the same time they are more than that, encompassing social relations. They provide a framework within which society has to operate and the structures within which society is located. They impose certain rules on society such as the natural 'laws' but at the same time they are part of a process of social construction. This means they exist independently of society although they are conceived of through a process of social construction. Therefore it is useful to make a distinction between ecological and social rhythms as expressions of time.

Social activity can change environmental rhythms through the interruption or change of ecological cycles. Social activity impacting on environmental processes can especially be found in the industrial sector, particularly mechanical and technological processes. This is one area where society is estranged from its relationship with the environment. The age of mass production and consumption, and the distanciation of the production process from the resource extraction stage has obscured the link between production, consumption, and environmental degradation, thus making it difficult to create a directly observable link between the accumulation of capital and the creation of environmental degradation. This is a problem that can be found in all forms of capitalism but becomes most acute with the technologies arising out of the industrial revolution:

> An advanced fossil fuel-based economy is very technology-centered apart from being environmentally degrading. However, ecological and technological processes do not share the same underlying principles according to which they evolve or function. Ecological processes are highly interactive, rhythmic, cyclical and 'renewable'. Technological processes, on the other hand, are extremely linear (i.e. non-renewable after their life span expires, and also producing high-entropy waste). Although some social technological processes can be interactive and rhythmic, technological products used in the production process certainly are not. A machine's life is mechanical and non-renewable, i.e. functions according to Newtonian principles (Adam & Kütting, 1995: 243).

Therefore, two worlds based on opposing principles have to cohabit, namely the environment and globalizing society based on mass production and consumption. Following the basis of ecological economics arguments, this means that industrial society is out of tune with the rhythms of nature, or ecosystems, and thus disturbs careful ecological balances by depositing non-renewable waste products on the planet, which diminish the available resources, or energy, on earth (Daly, 1996; Guha & Martinez-Alier, 1997; Martinez-Alier, 1999). This phenomenon can be summarized by distinguishing between mechanism and organism. Mechanical systems such as machine-based production societies draw on Newtonian concepts and assumptions. A mechanical view of nature implies that nature/environment can be neatly compartmentalized into constituent parts and that these parts are not interdependent, or only interdependent at the clearly observable level. This approach likens its worldview to a car engine in which a broken part can be fixed and the engine will work again because the functions of the broken part are clearly visible and thus repair is easy and straightforward. An organic view of the world, on the other hand, can be described as focusing on the connections and dependent relations of nature, thus stressing the holistic aspect. This view also highlights the cyclical, evolutionary, and irreversible nature of environmental rhythms. Connections here are not as clearly visible as in the car engine and effects of a 'broken part' can be felt in places and at times that cannot be traced back in a direct line to the original disturbance.

There is no doubt that human activity brings about environmental change just as the invasion of sub-Saharan plains by elephants does. As human activity has become highly commodified under systems of mass production or intense economic activity, this usually takes a toll in changing and degrading ecological processes. This can have far-reaching consequences as in the case of the ship-building industry in classical Greece and the resulting deforestation of the Mediterranean or through the development of a fossil fuel economy resulting in industrialization. This leads to changes in the ecosystem and the ecosystem may change as a result. This change does not necessarily constitute (global) environmental degradation although it may lead to some temporary local degradation. The grouping together of human beings in settlements will always lead to environmental change. Environmental change in itself may have deleterious side effects but does not constitute environmental degradation in itself. However, environmental degradation takes place when the constant amount of energy existing on the planet is transformed into irretrievable forms of energy and waste. Such entropic changes are essentially the result of the overexploitation of renewable resources such as soil or forests or water, or the result of the use of non-renewable energy and its transformation into waste such as the burning of fossil fuels (Daly, 1996).

These definitions of the structural origins of environmental degradation can be supplemented with an understanding of the nature of rhythms. Ecological rhythms are largely a cyclical phenomenon. However, hegemonic social conceptions of time are linear. Therefore, there seems to be an incompatibility between social and ecological rhythms of time. Since human beings are part of nature and the larger physical environment, this clash of concepts leads to questions on the effect of an 'unnatural' (i.e., social) rhythm on the larger physical environment. However, this identification of two separate rhythmic phenomena and the isolation of social rhythms from the rhythms of the larger physical environment mean that mass-producing society has distanced itself from ecological rhythms, either consciously or as an unintended consequence of other processes.

This distancing is a phenomenon that can be found both in the social relations within the hegemonic North as well as in the social relations between the developed and the developing world. The social, political, and economic control of the different notions of time, or timescapes as Barbara Adam calls it (1998), determines the organization of society but also has fundamental consequences for the relations between environment and society with often unplanned, unintended, and unforeseeable consequences for society. This also applies to the globalizing of production where the spatial and temporal relations under neoliberalism are witness to a new era of finance and property relations. These new relations in turn lead to a new rhythmicity in the relations between social and ecological time from a global perspective. A fundamental aspect of these global temporal social and ecological structures is the issue of time-space distanciation. This subject has traditionally been analyzed with a social or economic focus but has a strong environmental dimension as well.

TIME-SPACE DISTANCIATION

This aspect of the temporal discussion focuses on one of the cornerstones of globalization debates, namely the concept of time-space distanciation. The basic idea behind this concept is that under globalization social relations are spatially removed, creating global-local linkages through economic and cultural practices (Giddens, 1990). At the same time social relations are also temporally removed in two ways: first of all, events can be experienced simultaneously in different places through sophisticated technology and, second, the consequences of an action or policy may not be felt in a different place until sometime after the actual events (temporal distanciation). So, time-space distanciation is mostly about global-local linkages. A good example of time-space distanciation is the ozone hole. The current ozone hole over Latin America, Australia, and Antarctica is caused by the production, consumption, and resulting release into the atmosphere of ozone-depleting substances produced and released over thirty years ago in mostly industrialized countries.

Time-space separation disconnects social activity from its particular social context as can be seen in the field of food production. This distanciation is manifested in many developing countries by the growing of cash crops for global markets rather than for the satisfaction of local dietary needs (and the import of food crops for urban populations). It will become even more manifest when plant life can be patented and indigenous plant genes will be 'owned' by commercial enterprises elsewhere in the word (Miller, 2001). In industrialized countries, spatial distance is best expressed by the seasonally unaffected diet of consumers as dictated by supermarket shopping. This distanciation leads to a breakaway from local cultural activities and habits and a move toward 'disembedded' institutions, which can be economic, social, or cultural. Redclift sees the main effect of time-space distanciation in the confusion between intention, action, and outcome (1996: 147). This means that time-space distanciation leads to difficulties in establishing causal links between actions and their consequences. As David Goodman and Michael Redclift argue with respect to the international food system: "With the simultaneous access to geographically separate production zones, the formation of the world market freed industrial capitals from the seasonality of individual national agricultures, approximating the continuous production process characteristic of industry" (1991: 96). The consequences of this phenomenon are enormous for the understanding of solutions to the problem of environmental degradation. It shows that economic and regulatory structures are 'disembedded' and not equipped, thus not able, to adequately address environmental problems. It also shows that events or actions in one part of the globe are either the unintended consequences of actions elsewhere or the deliberate but disconnected results of actions elsewhere.

Second, time-space distanciation provides the foundation for the rise of what Giddens calls the rationalized organization and that Weber associated with bureaucracy. However, even more than the inertia criticized by Weber, modern rational organizations are characterized by a dynamism on the local-global level that was unthinkable in Weber's age. This has also been recognized by Paul Virilio and James Der Derian in their respective discussions of speed (Virilio, 1986; Der Derian, 1992). Not only has the distinction between time and place decreased in importance but as a related phenomenon the velocity of change and progress has increased exponentially in the latter half of the twentieth century. Changes in the global division of labor and in the production structure leading to 'just in time' manufacturing and to the practice of subcontracting in the production process in order to achieve maximum flexibility vis-à-vis unpredictable consumer demand are cases in point (Klein, 2000).

Third, the notion of history has changed fundamentally with the rise of these rationalized organizations. Unitary standards of measuring time ensure a universality of history and with the universal mapping of the planet, 'time and space are recombined to form a genuinely world-historical framework of action and experience" (Giddens, 1990: 21). However, this universalist vision of history is that of the benefactors of time-space distanciation, namely the enterprises and governments with the resources to overcome the time-space compression. In addition to universalizing history, the discussion of time-space distanciation refers to changes in the production structure of social organization but neglects to study the effects of this distanciation on the environment. It is especially in the area of environment-society relations that the time-space distanciation, particularly its temporal aspects, has changed dramatically with the rise and development of the various forms of capitalism. An extension of the concept of this distanciation to environmental matters is vital since social organization does not exist in an environmental vacuum and society is dependent on natural resources and sinks for its survival. The next section will look at the institutional framework that regulates this distanciation and other phenomena. Although the structural origins of environmental degradation are the primary concerns of this chapter, it is also important to look at governance issues managing these problems as they are part of social structures dealing with environmental degradation. However, governance and trade issues are seen as a subordinate structure to the three main strands of this book and will be discussed in the context of each strand in this and chapters 3 and 4 rather than as separate entitites.

GLOBAL GOVERNANCE

Global governance is an umbrella term covering different types of international or transnational regulation or institutionalization. So, for example, regimes are seen as a traditional form of global governance and so are international institutions such as the World Trade Organization (WTO) or the United Nations (UN). Recently, transnational forms of governance have also been included in this definition such as global codes of conducts used by multinational corporations or by the development of norms by global civil society. There is global political and economic governance. The number of global governance institutions has risen dramatically in the past thirty years or so and with increasing trade and financial regulation, these areas have been opened up for global institutionalization and removed from the domestic arena. As James Rosenau puts it:

> Governance is a more encompassing phenomenon than government. It embraces governmental institutions but it also subsumes informal, nongovernmental mechanisms, whereby those persons and organizations within its purview move ahead, satisfy their needs, and fulfill their wants. . . . Governance is thus a system of rule that is as dependent on intersubjective meanings as on formally sanctioned constitutions and charters. . . . It is possible to conceive of governance without government—of regulatory mechanisms in a sphere of activity which function effectively even though they are not endowed with formal authority (Rosenau & Czempiel, 1992).

In the environmental field, the number of international environmental agreements and voluntary arrangements is well in the hundreds and covering all sorts of regional and global issues ranging from the Kyoto Protocol to forest stewardship councils. However, even more important is the relationship between economic and environmental governance and the lack of environmental provisions in the economic sphere or the precedence economic institutions and regulations take over environmental ones (Conca, 2000; M. Weber, 2001).

In the field of global governance a variety of actors, structures, and regulations converge and need to be separated for heuristic purposes although they obviously form a coherent (or not so coherent) whole. There are a number of global governance organizations that are closely related to global environmental governance. These are the environmental institutions of the UN but, more importantly, non-environmental organizations such as the WTO, the (International Monetary Fund), IMF and the World Bank have a strong impact on environmental governance through their economic, trade, investment, and development policies. I will not cover the role of international environmental agreements that is mostly put into practice through UN agencies here as I have done so in great detail elsewhere and have where I demonstrated that these agreements are fairly marginal to global environmental governance from an eco-holistic perspective (Kütting, 2000).

Global economic and political governance, which structurally determines environmental governance, leads to the sidelining of ecological considerations and a disregard of environment-society relations. This means that global governance takes place in the absence of an understanding of social dependence on ecological foundations. Thus it can be explained that the absence of environmental priorities in the WTO as the main system of global economic governance is more indicative of global environmental governance than the drafting of international environmental agreements on particular issue areas that are negotiated under the constraints of this global institutional economic framework. Likewise, the structural adjustment policies of the World Bank and the International Monetary Fund have a strong environmental message through the role that is being apportioned to environmental considerations in this development framework. Although the World Bank has put environmental policy high on its agenda, this has been done in a sustainable development framework that assumes unlimited growth and denies the basic realities of environmental equity and resource access (Williams, 2001; M. Miller, 1995).

A large part of the academic debate on global governance focuses on the changing role of the state in the international system and its potential replacement by other actors and the decline of sovereignty. In the words of Ronnie Lipschutz:

> One of the central issues facing human civilization at the end of the 20th century is governance: Who rules? Whose rules? What rules? What kind of rules? At what level? In what form? Who decides? On what basis? Many of the problems that give rise to questions such as these are transnational and transboundary in nature, with the result that the notion of global 'management' has acquired increasing currency in some circles. This is especially true given that economic globalization seems to point toward a single integrated world economy in which the sovereign state appears to be losing much of its authority and control over domestic and foreign affairs (1999: 259).

The debate about the loss of sovereignty of the state is one of the main cornerstones of globalization studies although from a critical global political economy perspective, it may make more sense to talk of a transfer of power or political division of labor. Although it may seem that states are losing power, they are still the only sovereign actors in the international system and they are the actors who have put into place (and govern) the very institutions that are supposed to challenge the power of the state. It seems that rather than declining, the power of the Northern or industrialized state is actually fortified through the global economic governance institutions that at the end of the day represent the interests of the haves against the have-nots. From this point of view, plus ça change plus c'est la même chose. It is actually the power of the developing country state that is being undermined by global governance or rather prevented from developing as most developing countries have never been in a position of structural power. Therefore the global economic institutions can be seen as the exercise of structural power rather than as the decline of the power of the state.

It is clearly obvious that the global politico-economic framework legitimized by states and global institutions provides a formidable system for the efficient transfer of resources from the periphery to the core and thus provides a continuation of more violent or more directly exploitative policies of the past. At the same time, despite the increasing environmental rhetoric in the form of the sustainable development discourse (Redclift, 1987), there has been no real attempt to take onboard the strained nature of environment-society relations and consequently there has been no real effort to accommodate environmental with social needs.

The disillusionment with state policies and international organizations has led to the rise of transnational protest movements and to the rise of non-governmental actors in both the civil society and corporate fields (although a strict definition of civil society includes the corporate sector, modern usage of the term suggests a distinction). These civil society actors have been busy creating additional and alternative forms of global governance that have become part of the global network of regulations, norms, and ethics (Schweitz, 2001). In some cases, they contribute to and shape international governance; in some cases transnational governance exists in addition to international governance (Keck & Sikkink, 1998; Princen and Finger, 1994).

Global corporate governance takes place on two levels. First of all, the rise of the multinational corporation has drawn after it the increasing liberalization of trade and finance institutionalized through international organizations (Newell, 2001). These are structural changes leading to a different corporate climate and can thus be described as a type of corporate governance although the corporate entity is obviously not the legitimator of this governance. Second, multinational corporations have set up among themselves certain rules they abide by as a form of self-governance. There is a multilayered rationale to this self-governance (Hein & Fuchs, 1999). First of all, self-governance delays or avoids the imposition of other rules, which may be stricter, compulsory, or less convenient. Second, self-governance facilitates standardization that is good for expansion but also for monopolization. Third, self-governance is good for the image. Typical forms of self-governance are, for example, the International Standards Organization (ISO) is not an international governmental organization and that develops voluntary standards such as ISO 9001 and ISO 14001, which are procedural and environmental procedural standards, respectively. Corporate codes of conducts as found in the garment industry and as highlighted by the Gap and Nike are another form of self-governance. These standards have been introduced as apparel companies came increasingly under attack for the atrocious working conditions under which their garments were produced, usually by subcontractors. These voluntary codes of conduct designed by the companies themselves commit companies to patroling working conditions in the factories where their garments are made and where the companies themselves are responsible for their implementation. From this point of view they can be described as the fox guarding the chicken coop but in the absence of enforceable legislation, these codes of conduct are at least an admission that these activities need to be regulated. So, global corporate governance has facilitated the establishment of global markets but has so far avoided the regulation of social and environmental degradation.

There has been a very strong response to this increasing global corporate climate and market-based governance from the global civil society quarters (Lipschutz, 2001b). Global civil society contributes to, and tries to reform, other forms of governance. The rationale behind this is that the Northern or Western state has increasingly given up on its social welfare role and becomes a representative or guardian of the interests of global markets and therefore the 'police officer role' previously fulfilled by states has been increasingly taken over by non-state actors. Consequently, these actors are given a role in the international arena. Non-governmental organizations have an advisory role in the formulation and negotiation of international environmental agreements and are increasingly included in the advisory policy-making process of organizations such as the World Bank or the UN. They also have a role at the national level and feed into the policy process by advising foreign, development, and environment ministries. Non-governmental organizations involved in such formal channels are usually reformist rather than radical organizations. Radical organizations do not participate in shaping global governance because they believe that there are fundamental systemic shortcomings and that these cannot be addressed through a reform of existing forms of global governance. Radical movements can therefore be found outside the policy process in the form of the landless movement, protests outside WTO ministerial meetings, etc. (Goldman, 1998). The increasingly vocal nature and huge numbers of people involved in such movements have led to a questioning of the legitimacy of some forms of global governance and have thus had a result, albeit not an immediately tangible one (Conca, 2000).

To conclude, in terms of environment-society relations, the global governance process has become more pluralistic as a result of globalization but this has not necessarily led to increased consideration of environmental necessities at the global level. Although there are several groups of actors and institutions that are working in the environmental arena, this happens in subordination to the system of global economic governance and thus it can be said that a system of global environmental management exists but not a system of global environmental governance.

TRADE

The proliferation of trade is seen as the most visible sign of a globalizing economy. It is disputed whether the current time or the late nineteenth century have seen the largest volume of trade proportionately (Hirst & Thompson, 1996) but in any case, the institutionalization of trade liberalization can be seen as one of the engines of a globalizing political economy. Trade takes on an environmental dimension not just as a particular, ever-increasing branch of production but through the creation of environmental degradation by the shipping of products and services around the world.

From this perspective, an environmental trade distinction can be made between those products that are traded because they are not easily available in some parts of the world such as agricultural produce and those products that are traded although they are available in many parts of the world. The first category would, for example, be bananas or cotton or oil and the second category would be apples or beef or automobiles. These examples show that contemporary trade has nothing to do with the traditional law of comparative advantage or efficiency gains but is the result of liberal market ideology and the struggle for market shares.

More trade and more transport of goods means more economic activity and thus more profit, more employment, and more competition. This can then result in such situations as the famous German yogurt whose ingredients had circled the globe once in terms of miles accumulated until their final destination. Anomalous situations from an environmental perspective can also be seen in the import of New Zealand apples to Britain during the British apple season or the availability of foreign plain yogurts or milk in supermarkets when there is a farming surplus in the United Kingdom. This raises two questions, first a question about the compatibility of trade and the environment and second a normative question about ethics and choice; Where should the line be drawn between consumer choice and environmental considerations?

These questions cannot be addressed in an intellectual vacuum. In the age of globalization a commitment to freer trade and trade liberalization is the framework within which analysis takes place. Although there can be no question about the fact that the global and international trade institutions subordinate ecological considerations to the principle of uninhibited trade and are thus substantial contributors to disturbed environment-society relations, trade and the environment need to be analyzed with at least some reference to this institutional framework (see, e.g., M. Weber, 2001).

As Hemmer puts it, albeit from an environmental management and pre-WTO perspective:

> ... One may wonder whether trade liberalization within the framework of the GATT [General Agreement on Tariffs and Trade] and sustainable development are compatible. Trade liberalization is not necessarily incompatible with the objectives of environmental policy. On the contrary, if one supposes advanced environmental policies, it may be argued that sustainable environmental conditions are impossible to achieve without appropriate incentives to enhance the efficiency of resource use. But sustainable development also implies that restrictions have to be imposed on the levels and methods of natural resources exploitation. Thus, trade-offs exist between trade liberalization and environmental protection. In practice this may lead to conflicts. Whereas the GATT aims at deregulation of international trade, national environmental policies use instruments that regulate trade, such as licenses, product standards, levies and subsidies. . . . Hence, it may be argued that trade liberalization should follow two paths simultaneously. One is the removal of trade barriers that obstruct and distort trade and prevent efficient resource use. The other is the use of non-distortive environmental and trade instruments that favor sustainable resource use in a non-discriminatory way (1992: 19).

Hemmer raises an important point here, namely that in certain situations free trade can actually lead to environmental improvement. Would this then mean that it makes more sense to have a global environmental framework for trade instead of national rules and norms? However, the experience of international environmental agreements shows that a global framework would be one of the lowest common denominator.

It should not be forgotten that although we live in an age of trade liberalization, world trade is far from free. Only a limited range of products and services enjoy trade liberalization and ironically precisely the agricultural market, where developing countries can compete with developed countries, is where trade is still heavily regulated and biased in favor of the heavily subsidized Northern countries, as the case of cotton presented in chapter 6 so aptly illustrates. Trade in textiles is also a case in point (Cortes, 1997). Protected markets through regional economic integration organizations and agricultural subsidies give a distorted picture of agricultural trade. Thus, the global institutional trade framework seems to be geared toward supplying consumer elites with a large and favorably priced range of products through an arbitrary interpretation of the free trade ideology.

Trade per se cannot be seen as an environmental evil except by some radical ecologists who would rather not produce anything and become hunter-gatherers again as the least environmentally degrading food procurement activity. Excessive trade, on the other hand, is a major environmental problem. The question of when trade becomes excessive trade is an ideological question and will differ from one perspective to the next. However, it is also a question that is not asked in the sustainable development or trade liberalization discourses. Trade is also an equity issue that cannot be separated from the environmental problématique. If a perfect ecologically sound global society was one without trade, would that not make it impossible for technologically challenged states to develop the sort of infrastructure to close the gap? Likewise, without trade most consumer goods could not be made as their components/ingredients come from all over the world. What would the implications of this be?

Trade has existed for thousands of years, both in a barter and a monetary economy. Therefore the classical argument of environmental degradation arising out of the rise of modern capitalism and the ensuing increase in trade cannot be correct. Thus, the argument of trade being a major cause of environmental degradation would work better in an ecological world systems theory approach.

However, it can be argued that not trade liberalization per se leads to the rise of excessive trade but the liberalization of capital and finance that has then drawn after itself a rise in trade. The free movement of capital and money has led to the rise of intrafirm trade, which after all makes up 75 percent of global trade (Hirst & Thompson, 1996). Likewise, the increasingly complex and global capital ownership patterns and the rise of foreign direct investment are the underlying sources of trade expansion and the developing institutional trade framework is merely a response to this trend. As such it does not make any explicit reference to environment and it can be argued that many of the structural problems in environment-society relations can be traced back to this issue.

CONCLUSION

In this chapter, I have analyzed environment-society relations in the period of a globalizing political economy. Environmental degradation per se is nothing new and not specific to globalizing tendencies. In fact, forms of environmental degradation can be found under all fairly sophisticated forms of for-profit production. However, the achievements of the industrial revolution in terms of technological advances and the evolution of a fossil fuel economy and thus the move from renewable to non-renewable forms of energy have seen a globalizing of environmental degradation whereas before degrading effects were largely local or regional.

Thus, on the one hand, the relationship between environment and globalization seems to be a continuum of the relationship between capitalism and the environment as such. On the other hand, at a closer look, important new distinctions can be drawn out. There are many dimensions to environment-society relations that are new under a globalizing political economy.

Essentially, environment-society relations under globalization are shaped by the tenets of neoliberal ideology and by the liberalization of production and finance. This liberalization and its supporting institutional framework have led to a new form of ecological imperialism that subjugates resource extraction and production to market ideology. Although 'exploitation' can be found in previous forms of capitalism and particularly colonialism, there is a new element to this in globalization as there is a declining interest in looking after resources for future use since production can move on and exploit another part of the world when one area has been exhausted. This problem is particularly relevant for developing countries and developed countries tend to be the recipients and benefactors of this system, having greater consumer choice and competitive prices.

This disenfranchising of local control is supported by the system of global governance and trade that has been institutionalized in support of neoliberal ideology and supports its smooth functioning. There can be no doubt that the global politico-economic framework legitimized by states and global institutions provides a formidable system for the efficient transfer of resources from the periphery to the core and thus provides a continuation of more violent or more directly exploitative policies of the past. At the same time, despite the increasing environmental rhetoric in the form of the sustainable development discourse, there has been no real attempt to take onboard the strained nature of environment-society relations and consequently there has been no real effort to accommodate environmental with social or societal needs. Although there is a sustainable development discourse, an ever-increasing number of international environmental agreements and environmental provisions are included in trade agreements, these efforts can at best be seen as efforts to manage environmental problems, and at worst as eyewash supposed to placate those who criticize the hegemonic practices.

Chapter 3

Cultural versus Political Economy Approaches: Production and Consumption

This chapter will be concerned with another core type of globalization literature that has received little attention in the International Relations (IR) field
but nevertheless makes an important contribution to the literature and practice
of globalization. The cultural aspect of globalization has a historical and
material perspective in that transnational cultural influences can be traced
back to the evolution of empires, the spread of organized religion, and forces
such as colonialism, and ideological diffusion. These social forces complement economic processes of globalization and are intrinsically linked with
them. The nature and form of capitalism is culturally as well as economically
and politically informed. The notion of culture through the institution of
consumption and its influence on the global political economy will be discussed in this chapter. This debate about production and consumption constitutes the second pillar around which the eco-holistic approach to Global
Political Economy (GPE) is built. The main argument here is that GPE is
production-centric and needs to take more account of the institution of consumption. This is packaged in the wider argument of culture/consumption
versus political economy/production. While discounting the need for more
cultural approaches, the need for a more consumption-aware analysis of GPE
is illustrated here by showing the glaring need for a more consumption-
focused outlook from an eco-holistic perspective.

Culture is a fuzzy concept to define and mainly refers to social practices
and beliefs that are rooted in particular forms of religious, social, economic,
and political practices predominant in a society. It is also a predominantly
Western concept and can be found in Western literature on sociology and
social and political theory. In fact, cultural globalization is often equated with
the spread of Western social and cultural practices at the global level, often
through multinational corporations such as 'McDonaldization' or through
the spread of Western media and entertainment culture. However, such a
concept of cultural globalization would not constitute globalization but rather

Westernization. In fact, in the West/North consumption is seen as a cultural phenomenon as it is the key instrument through which culture is represented and reproduced (Miles, 1998: 3; Sklair, 2002: chapters 5 and 7).

Another aspect of cultural globalization is the increasing popularity and spread of particular fashions that lead to a global consumer class. It is manifested by the spread of brand names that are globally known and recognizable (Klein, 2000). This is both an economic and a cultural phenomenon and a form of manufactured culture. By this I mean that it is an attempt to manufacture a particular type of 'global citizen' that it is desirable to aspire to. This is not an evolved form of culture but an attempt at artificially creating a transnational cultural type that is predominantly characterized by the consumption of global brand names and a particular form of news and entertainment (Klein, 2000; Sklair, 2002). However, in fact, again, this is not global culture but the spread of one particular type of Western consumption pattern. It is also not a cultural but an economic phenomenon.

Given the intrinsic linkage between political economy and cultural phenomena, it is very difficult to make a case for either factor as a singular engine for world development. Since economic, political, and social practices are culturally informed and as culture is determined by the economic and social makeup of a society, the two can only heuristically be separate. For this reason, many historical materialists or political economists have tended to ignore the subject of culture as it is seen as being covered by the focus on political economy. However, there is more to culture than that and global culture is not the spread of Starbucks coffee and Nike trainers, the global popularity of Harry Potter, or the use of English as a global language. Likewise, global culture is not the availability of Ethiopian food in U.S. restaurants or the global appeal of reggae or salsa music. The spread of Western consumer goods cannot be described as global culture and the use of English as a global language is historically determined. Culture refers to social practices and how they influence belief systems and therefore political and economic practices. This is not how the sociology globalization writers see culture; therefore, a disciplinary distinction needs to be drawn.

Roland Robertson, for example, says that "For the most part, the debate about culture among sociologists has been expressed along remarkably mechanical lines; by which I mean that the debate has continued in terms of choices between whether culture is more or less determined and whether it is determinative" (1992: 45). This is not a debate that can be found in the International Relations/International Political Economy (IPE) field of globalization studies. From this perspective, culture is seen as a contributory factor to the socio-economic determinants of society rather than as a driving force behind social relations itself.

An emphasis on culture is predominantly found in reflectivist and particularly in post-modern approaches to social science rather than in rationalist theories. These approaches are geared toward exploring the socially constructed nature of social practices and are therefore very open toward the concept of culture as an influential explanatory variable as culture can ideally explain different social values across spatial or temporal boundaries. Most political economy approaches, on the other hand, are still firmly entrenched in the rationalist field although they do take limited account of the nature of social construction.

On the subject of culture and environment, literature in the field of IR or IPE/GPE has been extremely limited and the subject has mostly received attention in a sociological or post-modern/post-structuralist context (Conley, 1997). However, for an environmentally informed study of globalization processes, an awareness of the culturally perceived notion of environment is crucial. A definition of environment, environmental change, and environmental degradation is culturally dependent as environmental values and environment-society relations are culturally, historically, and geographically specific. Likewise, the social construction of environment is not a global but rather a culturally specific undertaking that is linked to the direct experience of environmental degradation. At the moment, both the cultural and environmental dimensions of global political economy approaches are underdeveloped and need to be integrated further. However, this also means that the integration of culture and environment from an environmental GPE perspective is the least developed of all. Although this shortcoming will be marginally touched upon in this book, it is not the main focus of the project developed here.

CULTURE AS CONSUMPTION

One way to integrate a more culturally determined perspective into the political economy of globalization is to use the vehicle of consumption. In the historical materialist school of thought it is generally accepted that economic development from all angles is dependent on, and can be traced back to, production (Wallerstein, 1986, R. Cox, 1996). Globalization is thus traced back to changes in the production structure, to use Susan Strange's useful term (Strange, 1988, 1996, 1998). Consumption is the final destination of all that is produced. This means that both production and consumption activities today are more pervasive than at any other time because in the past twenty years world output has nearly trebled and this has obviously led to unprecedented levels of consumption (World Development Indicators, 2000: 188). The academic literature in global political economy has concentrated on analyzing production as the driving vehicle of progress and explanatory variable of social relations and has seen the activity of consumption as a natural extension of this production structure rather than as a social force or activity in its own right (Boyer & Drache, 1996; Hoogvelt, 1997; Hirst & Thompson, 1996; Dicken, 1992). This means that the study of consumption has been neglected and is one of the least understood economic activities.

Production and consumption are thus treated as more or less identical phenomena since we consume what we produce and vice versa. However, since our consumption volume has increased exponentially over the past 100 to 200 years with the rise of modern capitalism, there must be an origin to this production/consumption explosion and this has a cultural linkage. This origin is usually explained through the increased production capability of changes relating to the industrial revolution and consequently to changing social configurations. It would be circular to argue that increased production triggered more consumption or vice versa as demand for more consumer goods and thus more production must have been triggered by a change in social relations or by a special event (Campbell, 1987). This is an explanatory problem that the historical materialist approaches have not considered. However, it is a question of fundamental importance as the origin of the production and consumption increases under early modern capitalism is really the key to understanding the social behavior underlying the transition of this historical period and today's international system as well as the society we live in.

Consumption as a subject matter has traditionally been left to cultural studies and to sociology researchers and has not been regarded as a political economy subject. Consumption is viewed as a natural extension of production and so closely linked to it that it is considered sufficient to study production in order to understand larger political economy phenomena as Diane Perrons argues from this perspective:

> Consumption opportunities are profoundly shaped by material well-being, which in turn remains dependent both on an individual's positioning within the social relations of production, including the gender division of labor, and on their societies' position within the international division of labor (1999: 92).

However, such a perspective reduces consumption to the actual consuming of goods or services and to the consumer's place in the division of labor rather than integrating consumption as an integral part of social, political, economic, and environmental analysis. Consumption is not only the last stage of the production process but a phenomenon in its own right that influences the production process in more ways than creating demand. It also raises normative questions about the nature of the global political economy and about the nature of the economic system. It can address many issues such as equity, social justice, and general North-South issues that are sidelined in traditional analysis through a lack of conceptual tools adequate for holistic incorporation. Consumption is a sociological as well as an economic institution (Comor, 1998) and this socio-cultural aspect has direct and salient repercussions on the global political economy. It could be argued that the global economic changes that have occurred since the 1970s have coincided with fundamental changes in the consumer ethic in Western industrialized societies, which in turn have led to fundamental changes in the global division of labor. These changes have had negative social consequences as well as further exacerbating environmental degradation and obscuring nature-society relations. Therefore it is important to define consumption more widely than just as a natural extension of the production process or in the context of the international or global division of labor.

In order to comprehend the origins of these social and environmental shortcomings in the global political economy, it is necessary to consider the structure and recent changes in global production methods and global economic organization. As Baudrillard argues with reference to poverty rather than to general and environmental degradation (but equally applicable here):

> If poverty and nuisance cannot be eliminated, this is because they are anywhere but in the poor neighborhoods. They are not in the slums or shanty-towns but in the socio-economic structure. Yet this is precisely what has to be concealed, what must not be said and indeed billions of dollars are spent on hiding the fact (1998: 56).

This point can be extended further to the issue of consumption. It is not just the nature of production but also the nature of consumption that leads to economies of flexibility, conceals fundamental inequalities, and perpetuates patterns of environmental degradation. In a world where 20 percent of the global population consume 80 percent of the world's resources (Sachs et al., 1998: 48ff.) it will not be sufficient to adopt international environmental norms that provide technical solutions to environmental problems, or that aim to increase the amount of disposable income among citizens of developing countries (Kütting, 2000). There exists a fundamental problem about the limited availability of resources and access to these and this problem is obscured by the nature of the globalization discourse. By bringing in the phenomenon of consumption and by raising questions about the ethic of consumption, this focus can be substantially broadened leading to a more holistic approach. Thus it is possible to go beyond the narrow analytical passageways provided by the environmental literature that takes a very functional approach to consumption in terms of scarcity of resources and the globalization literature that sees globalization firmly rooted in the production sector.

THE HISTORY OF PRODUCTION AND CONSUMPTION

As discussed in chapter 1, there are several explanations for the globalizing of the political economy and they are located in various time frames. All of these explanations relate to production methods or modes. Especially within IR, historicist approaches have tended to focus on international commerce as the motor of development and thus the (domestic) institution of consumption was not part of analytical frameworks (Agnew, 1993: 23).

There are two notable exceptions to this state of affairs, in the fields of sociology and history respectively. Colin Campbell (1987) argues that the rise of a romantic and a Protestant ethic coincides with the evolution of the spirit of modern consumerism. Neil McKendrick, John Brewer, and J. H. Plumb (1982) talk about the consumer revolution and the commercialization of economics, particularly in the field of fashion. Furthermore, consumption has obviously been incorporated and quantified—but obviously not qualified—through the inclusion of 'demand' in the supply and demand curve in economics. Naturally, consumer preference is analyzed by marketing analysts and market researchers but these studies are not undertaken in a social context. Thus general social scientific attempts to conceptualize consumption have not really been a subject of inquiry in the political sciences.

This existing if sparse body of literature suggests that changes in consumerism can be equated with the rise of modern capitalism and that the evolution of a consumerist ethic contributed to the success of the industrial revolution and of modern modes of production. Likewise, a definite change in the ethics of consumption can be discerned in the 1960s and 1970s with the spread of Fordism, which in turn coincided with what is conceived of as the rise of globalization. There is no literature on the role of consumption in earlier forms of capitalism so this dimension cannot be explored in more detail here but will be explored further in chapter 4 with reference to origins of environmental degradation and to different types of consumerism as a possible structural origin.

The rise of modern capitalism has been blamed or used as an explanatory variable (mostly by historical materialists) for innumerable events, phenomena, social evils, or increases in social well-being through technological innovation. Many of these causal linkages do not hold the test of scrutiny, especially in the light of evidence of other, earlier forms of capitalism displaying many similar evils. However, in the absence of any literature on earlier periods in history linking consumer ethics/behavior and production patterns, this linkage will have to be accepted with the proviso that correlation is not (necessarily) causation. After all, mass production is not a phenomenon exclusive to modern capitalism.

Both Campbell and McKendrick et al. and his colleagues trace changes in consumption patterns in the late eighteenth century back to a shift in the nascent middle classes that aspired to emulate the spending behavior of the rich. The early industrial revolution produced consumer rather than capital goods and by the eighteenth century most people in Britain had moneyed income that they tended to spend on consumer goods (Campbell, 1987: 19-25). Although the phenomena of consumer spending and of emulating higher classes are not new in history, the changing income structure of early modern capitalism led to more disposable income in the middle classes. McKendrick sees the increasing pace of changing fashions as a key contribution to increased consumerism. Up to about 1750 women's fashion took decades or longer to change while between 1753 and 1757 fashion changed dramatically in the course of only four years and between 1776 and 1777 as well in the course of only one year (1982: 56). The enthusiasm to be in fashion permeated all spheres of society and was carefully manipulated by the fashion industry. This is a Western phenomenon as fashions in other parts of the world such as Japan, China, North Africa, or the Muslim countries remained virtually the same for hundreds of years (1982: 36).

One example where this connection is particularly obvious is in the case of commodity chain analysis. Although loosely based on world systems theory, this approach takes a linear view of the production process with consumption 'tagged on'. Thus, this approach is production-focused as all historical materialist approaches are, and by placing consumption at the last stage of the production process, it denies the interactive linkage between the two and also imposes an economic determinism on the subject matter. Nevertheless, commodity chains are a good analytical tool for tracing the global nature of the production process without which the nature of consumption cannot be understood.

COMMODITY CHAINS AND CONSUMPTION

This section is based on the concept of global commodity chain analysis that takes a commodity as the starting point for analyzing the political, economic, social and, to a much lesser extent, ecological linkages between the different production and consumption stages. Therefore commodity chain analysis is not exclusively concerned with the different stages of production in the life of a commodity per se but also places it in a social context.

Terence Hopkins and Immanuel Wallerstein describe commodity chains as networks 'of labor and production processes whose end result is a finished commodity' (1986: 159, quoted in Gereffi & Korzeniewicz, 1994). Thus, a global commodity chain comprises not only the different production processes from raw material to finished product but also links households, firms, states, and social actors across spatial and temporal boundaries and analyzes their relationship with each other. There are producer-driven and consumer-driven commodity chains. As Gereffi, Korzeniewicz, and Korzeniewicz elaborate:

> Specific processes or segments within a commodity chain can be represented as boxes or nodes linked together in networks. Each successive node within a commodity chain involves the acquisition and/or organization of inputs, labor power and consumption. The analysis of a commodity chain shows how production, distribution and consumption are shaped by social relations. . . . The global commodity chain approach promotes a nuanced analysis of world-economic spatial inequalities in terms of differential access to markets and resources (1994: 2).

Commodity chain analysis comprises a strong historical component in that it sees variances in the production process over time and it is generally a world-systems approach and can also be seen as a general historical materialist approach. As such, it obviously places its emphasis on production rather than on consumption and sees consumption primarily as a spatial issue in the context of unequal social relations. Another main pillar of commodity chain analysis is the focus on industry competitiveness and core-periphery relations. The dynamics of the world-system have to some extent been discussed in chapter 1 and will be related to the issue of consumption in the section on ethics and consumption. In general, the role of consumption in commodity chain analysis (both consumer and producer driven) is underrepresented as Gereffi, Korzeniewicz & Korzeniewicz argue:

> One theoretically relevant category is largely implicit but not sufficiently developed: households . . . neither of these variables can be fully addressed without a more substantial discussion of the organization and composition of households and the changing relationship of households to enterprises and states. At stake is not merely the issue of households as a source of labor. In the modern world-economy the organization and composition of households embodies the construction of consumption as well as processes of status group formation. Households are a principal site in the construction of identities and a global commodity chain approach must further elaborate this category to avoid missing a crucial analytical link (1994: 12).

Households as the primary venue of consumption are more or less integrated into commodity chain analysis as the final destination of the product but do not provide a theoretical input into the analysis itself. Thus commodity chain analysis takes a linear approach rather than letting the ethic of consumption through attitude changes, taste, social consciousness, etc. feed back into the production process. Consumption, or consumers/households are seen as the last link in the chain rather than as a structural force or agent influencing production or other social processes. This is one of the problems to be addressed for integrating consumption into commodity chains. Another problem closely related to consumption is the environmental or ecological aspect of commodity chains.

The commodity chain approach traditionally operates without locating itself in its environmental context. This means that it regards resources as inputs, disregards waste output, and sidelines the finite nature of resources and sinks. In short, it does not take account of the fact that the social construct of an economy is physically located within the global ecosystem and is dependent on drawing on its resources as well as on putting its waste into this system. The finite nature of the resources used for production as well as the fragile nature of the ecosystem as a recipient of waste products in the form of pollution are complicating factors that need to be incorporated into commodity chain analysis as they are also part of the chain. Thus commodity chain analysis needs to be placed in an ecological framework for holistic analysis.

It could be argued that part of this task is actually fulfilled in a life cycle analysis (LCA) approach but LCA is an environmental management approach while the study put forward here is based on an eco-holistic approach. Life cycle analysis 'measures the environmental impacts of products over their entire life cycle from cradle to grave' (Berkhout, 1997). Environmental management approaches such as LCA or regime analysis take the management of an environmental problem within existing institutional frameworks as their focus of analysis. This means that rather than starting off with the environmental problem and looking at its structural and social origins and the best possible ways of resolving the problem, these approaches start off with existing institutional and bureaucratic frameworks and study how these can best deal with the environmental problem. Therefore they try to fit the environmental problem into bureaucratic frameworks rather than defining the best way of dealing with the problem as institutional frameworks are too general to take account of the specific social and structural origins of an environmental problem (Kütting, 2000). Very often these structural origins can be traced back to the very institutional frameworks set up to deal with them. Therefore, environmental management approaches 'manage' environmental problems rather than resolve them.

Environmental management approaches thus fall into the category of what Cox refers to as problem-solving theory. In this context, the term problem-solving theory is misleading to the theoretically unaware as it gives the impression that it is geared toward solving a particular problem. According to Cox, problem-solving theory reproduces prevailing power and social relationships with the general aim of problem-solving being 'to make these relationships and institutions work smoothly by dealing effectively with particular sources of trouble' (1987: 128–129). An ecocentric or rather eco-holistic approach, on the other hand, goes beyond the study of institutions and critically assesses social practices leading to environmental degradation. Thus an eco-holistic approach could in some ways be described as a variant of critical theory in that it stands apart from prevailing orders and structures by not taking institutions and social/power relationships for granted and as the boundaries within which to think or act. Eco-holism incorporates the ecosystem within which global society is located as the starting point rather than studying society as if it was not located in, and dependent on, its natural environment.

To relate this point back to commodity chain analysis, there has been little attempt to incorporate this environmental dimension into this approach. There have been general approaches at ecological world-system theory such as Sing Chew's work but this does not look at commodity chains (2001). Therefore there is a need for a body of literature that brings together a form of critical life cycle analysis with commodity chain analysis. Such an approach would also need to incorporate the issue of consumption as the nature of consumption in the modern world-system and in the 'tyranny of consumption expectations' (Maniates, 2001), are clearly not compatible with the reality of a finite ecosystem. Thus the economic determinism of commodity chains needs to be broadened to include socio-economic and ecological considerations in order to be a truly inclusive analysis of labor and production networks. However, the transnational nature of commodity chain analysis offers excellent insights into the larger logic of global restructuring (Conca, 2001: 58).

THE GLOBAL DIVISION OF LABOR AND CONSUMPTION

Consumption is often reduced to the spending power of an individual that is dependent on their position within the division of labor. Therefore the increasingly global division of labor spatially distanciates the locations of production and consumption, meaning that there is no or only a distant relationship between the production and the consumption process. First I will discuss the changing division of labor and then I will consider the spatial distanciation between production and consumption and relate this back to changes in labor relations.

One of modern capitalism's main features is an advanced division of labor. In the twentieth century, this division of labor has been characterized by Taylorism, Fordism, and post-Fordism (Lipiètz, 1997: 2). All three models are based on making consumer goods available to a wider user circle through a revised wage structure and through mass production, making consumer goods cheaper.

While Taylorism was mainly about the streamlining of the production process, there was a more definite consumerist argument to Fordism. The idea behind Fordism was not only the automation of the production process but also making mass-produced consumer goods available to a wider base. The rationale was simple: there was a limited market for capital goods such as cars and that market would be exhausted fairly soon. Therefore new markets needed to be created and the logical solution was to make luxury consumer goods available to workers by reducing the prices through mass production and by increasing wages. Thus cars became available for much larger segments of society. In the 1950s and 1960s Fordism was also characterized by stable jobs for life, wage settlements that meant steadily increasing wages every year, a general rise in the standard of living, redistributive state policies, and institutionalized collective bargaining. These conditions secured an outlet for production and obviously led to drastically increased consumption behavior as households spent their income, as well as leading to vastly increased expectations in terms of standard of living.

However, this increase in consumption or the standard of living was limited to the developed world, and mostly to OECD countries. Although production was becoming internationalized at this stage, the consumer class was still almost exclusively situated in the North/West. At the end of the 1960s, markets in industrialized countries were slowly becoming saturated and consumer spending was down and profitability of companies went down as well (Mittelman, 1997). Logically, the perks of job security and ever-increasing wages in real terms could not be sustained in this period. Rather than expanding markets in the search for new consumers, other changes happened. As Hoogvelt summarizes:

> By the late 1960s that distinctive period of mass production and Fordist accumulation had come to an end. The rigidities of the Fordist regime showed up with irrepressible frequency. There were many instances of rigidity at all levels but the most important was undoubtedly the deepening global inequalities. These put a limit on the further expansion of that particular system of mass production. There was a global demand crisis and thus capitalism had to reconstitute

itself on an entirely new basis. In a world economy where 20 per cent of the population has 150 times the spending capacity of the poorest 20 per cent, clearly a new production system was needed that could fully exploit consumer demand from the 'have-lots' in an ever fiercer climate of global competition (1997: 93).

Enter the era of post-Fordism that is characterized by economies of flexibility. As a result of the economic instability of the 1970s workers in industrialized countries lost many of the perks they had quickly become accustomed to such as more or less permanent jobs, generous wage settlements, and social benefits. As Cox puts it: "The new strategies emphasized a weakening of trade union power, cutting of state budgets (especially for social policy), deregulation, privatization and priority to international competitiveness" (1996: 22). The new economic organization was much leaner and was based on maximizing profits. Ken Conca sees the post-Fordist mode of production to be based on flexible capital, vertical disintegration, and select markets, i.e., 'flexible specialization' (2001: 61). This was done not so much by broadening the consumer base but by making products cheaper and more easily available for those who had the spending power.

One crucial aspect of the post-Fordist mode of production is the availability of a global labor force. This has led to vastly increased insecurity at the workplace in developed countries, as put forward by Robert O'Brien: "Relatively secure labor in developed countries has been threatened by globalization as it has led to an undermining of the welfare state and intense competition from low wage producers" (2000: 538). Lower-wage structures and lack of costly worker safety or environmental regulations in some parts of the world can be utilized in order to keep the price of a particular product down. This means that the work force involved in the production process will not be able to afford the product it manufactures and has no relationship to it other than processing or producing it. Hence there is an increasing separation of the activities of production and consumption. Work forces become more temporary and in many circumstances there is a race to the bottom in terms of labor and wage standards and intense competition, particularly in South East Asia, takes place among the various labor forces for these flexible jobs in the spirit of 'it is better to be exploited than not to be exploited at all'. The demoralizing conditions in, for example, the textile sector in many developing countries will be treated in detail in section 2 of this book.

The post-Fordist flexible mode of production has not only led to a separation of the activities of production and consumption with the consequence that consumers are not aware of the ethical and environmental conditions under which the product they consume was made. It has also led to a further globalizing of production that is not matched by a globalized consumption pattern. This means that there is further polarization between different parts of the world with the high-earning jobs and consumption taking place in one place while production under flexible conditions has become global in many sectors. It can also be said that the production structure is set up in order to feed Northern/Western consumption patterns rather than to aim at increasing global consumption except for a transnational elite. Thus, the practicalities of an increasingly global division of labor show clearly that there now is an analytical distinction between production and consumption.

However, at the same time global institutions such as the World Bank, the International Monetary Fund (IMF), the World Trade Organization (WTO) and also the United Nations, etc. work toward achieving wealth for everybody through liberal and neoliberal policies and market dynamics. There seems to be a fundamental incompatibility between these two phenomena (see also Luke, 1998). The actual structure and practicality of the global institutional economic structure suggest that it serves the transnational elite as well as the Northern consumer; however, the rhetoric of such institutions calls for increased wealth for everybody.

CONSUMPTION AS AN ENVIRONMENTAL ISSUE

The environmental side of consumption is a major consideration for several reasons. First of all, the social and structural origins of environmental degradation can be found in the excessive consumption of the planet's resources. Second, the dominant neoliberal or even liberal approach in global management institutions is based on the assumption that the current standard of living enjoyed by the richest 20 per cent of the world population can be extended to the whole globe. In terms of resource availability, this is clearly a myth and leads to serious environmental and equity questioning. Third, consumption is not the last stage in the production chain; rather the last stage is disposal of the product consumed. Waste is a serious environmental problem not just for local authorities but globally and it affects the earth's capacity to act as a sink. All of these points will be developed in detail in the following section.

The argument that excessive consumption leads to environmental degradation is not a new argument and dates back to the late 1960s and early 1970s and to the beginnings of the environmental movement and to the 'Limits to Growth' report by the Club of Rome, a global think tank composed of scientists, economists, business people and heads of state. It is based on the 'need not want' philosophy. The early environmental movement in the 1970s questioned the ideology of consumerism in the period of unlimited expectations of the late 1960s and argued that the ideology of wanting more and more was fundamentally flawed and would lead to the ecological collapse of the planet. Rather, there should be an ideological shift to considering what people actually *needed* for a fulfilled life rather than *wanted*, i.e., a questioning of the ideology of unlimited economic growth and of an expected rise in the standard of living of those who had already achieved a high level. This movement coincided with the first oil crisis and with the first UN Conference for the Human Environment in Stockholm in 1972. The idea that there are insufficient resources has often been discredited with the discovery of new oil fields and with the introduction of more energy-efficient technologies that have pushed away the date when oil will run out from a predicted twenty years from the time of their writing to somewhere in the middle of the twenty-first century. Apart from the oil resources problem, there have been various predictions of disasters or shortages that have not come true. Gary Hardin's tragedy of the commons has not happened (1968) and the idea that an increasing world population cannot be fed with the agricultural resources of the planet has been discredited, thus also denying the need for genetically manipulated/modified crops. These are problems of distribution and access to resources rather than availability. Therefore the concern about running out of resources and the *need not want* campaign have lost their immediate urgency and have fizzled out

Alternative forms of creating energy have been developed and existing resources are being recycled. Technological advancements make it possible to find replacements for materials when the need arises. However, all of this does not change the fundamental truth that there is only a fixed amount of resources on this planet and although we are not in danger of running out just yet, these resources are being used up at an unsustainable rate by only a small part of the world population. What is more, it is not only a question of using up resources but also of degrading sinks, i.e., using ecosystems to deposit the wastes of the industrial production process.

The neoliberal economic order like its preceding economic orders treats the natural environment as if there was an unlimited supply of natural resources. The goods and services provided by the planet are not costed, unlike capital goods and resources owned by a supplier, and therefore they are externalized by economists and taken for granted in economic valuations. Environmental economists such as David Pearce have overcome this shortcoming by integrating previously 'free' goods into the economic system through price mechanisms but in essence this still does not change the fundamental paradox of externalizing the resource or energy supply that underlies social survival (Pearce, 1989, et al.). In addition, by pricing environmental goods they can become luxury goods and therefore only be available to those who can afford them. That often makes environmental quality a preserve of the rich rather than a human right and again raises questions of equity and access.

To come back to the subject of consumption and environment, no inhabitant of this planet has not been exposed to some form of environmental degradation and suffered a decline in conditions of living because of it and is therefore aware of the limited capacity of the planet to cope with the rate of extraction of resources and depositing of waste. Therefore the need for creating a careful balance between environmental and societal needs are abundantly clear and the link between an individual's pattern of consumption and environmental decline needs to be highlighted more, leading back to consumption, agency, and responsibility. However, even more important is the issue of environmental equity or environmental justice.

Environmental equity is a subject that has first made an appearance in the context of intergenerational equity meaning that each generation should pass on to the next generation a planet that can generate the means for survival. However, environmental equity is more than that. It is not just a question of equity over time but also equity across space. Under prevailing concepts of human rights based on a liberal consensus, all humans are equal and have an equal right to a decent standard of living. In practice, this cannot be realized although the principles of embedded liberalism imply that global institutions are in place to achieve an increase in the standard of living of the global poor. However, it has to be recognized that equal access to resources is a myth and will not happen without reconfigurations of power structures, or through market economics for that matter, and could only be achieved through a rethinking of approaches to environmental equity and justice.

As Fen Osler Hampson and Judith Reppy argue:

> We can conclude that the demands of social justice are inseparable from our responses to environmental change and our respect for the ecosystem: attention to one necessarily implicated the other. There is a general consensus . . . that traditional liberal theory is an imperfect framework for evaluating competing moral claims that arise in the context of environmental change. . . . A concern for social justice for individuals does not suffice when the cultural identity of the group is threatened. This is not to argue that the interests of the community or group should automatically trump the moral claims of the individual but simply to call for a theory of justice that allows communal values and future generations to be considered alongside the rights of the individuals living today (1996: 249).

The main thrust of this critique of liberal theory is that the overemphasis on the individual neglects the rights of groups such as indigenous communities or other societies. The emphasis on market instruments as the form of emancipation for the individual makes it difficult to consider group rights, especially in the case of indigenous communities. However, it has to be emphasized that classical liberalism had a strong moral component that safeguarded the rights of the weaker members of society. In the neoliberalism of the post-war world order these moral components are still intrinsically present but are employed in such a way that they are in fact ineffectual. For example, policies to integrate developing countries into the world economy are geared toward creating a middle (consumer) class in these countries through trade, FDI, etc. Such policies would then lead to a trickle down of the investment. So these policies are directed at benefiting individuals that would then create economic circumstances that would benefit society at large. No large-scale poverty alleviation is integrated into economic packages such as structural adjustment programs and IMF debt relief programs. The old argument of the relative versus the absolute benefit still applies and is very much relevant for the practical considerations of such policies.

The arguments made in favor of collective or societal responsibility and their equal status compared to the rights of the individual are points also made by Mike Maniates (2001). Maniates feels that the individualization of environmental responsibility is detrimental to the development of social institutions tackling the issue: "When responsibility for environmental problems is individualized, there is little room to ponder institutions, the nature and exercise of political power, or ways of collectively changing the distribution of power and influence in society—to, in other words, 'think institutionally' " (2001: 33). This may be a problem at the national level and the main problem here is the individualization of environmental problems at the expense of collective political responsibility of society. My argument operates at a different level and is in no way a call for the privatization of moral responsibility of the consumer. Rather, the argument for including the consumer as an actor in the global political economy and as a power entity is to be taken as an analytical and moral necessity for eco-holistic political economy research. A privatization of policy resulting in the sole responsibility on the consumer is neither desirable nor feasible as a consumer's choices are constrained by economic production frameworks. On the other hand, the sidelining of personal responsibility altogether as being practiced by IPE/GPE discourses is equally undesirable and that is why a political economy analysis of both productive and consumptive relations is necessary.

The argument that the issues of social justice and environmental degradation cannot be separated means that there are serious implications for the uneven pattern of consumption globally. If the current pattern of consumption in developed countries cannot be extended, at least hypothetically, to the global population, then clearly a redistribution of income is called for in order to share the existing resources more equitably in order to be in harmony with the principles of embedded liberalism. However, for debates on this subject to become pertinent, the myths of unlimited economic growth and of wealth for all need to be discredited first.

Last, not only is there a problem with uneven levels of consumption but also with the clearing up of excessive consumption. Consumer goods have a limited life span and then need to be disposed of by the consumer, in addition to the waste products that are unintended consequences of the production process. Commodity chain analysis or traditional environmental auditing undertaken by producers mostly does not take account of this last stage of the production/consumption process. Therefore the environmental cost of a product often does not reflect the whole ecological impact.

A veritable economy of waste has developed, especially in the field of toxic or nuclear waste. This trade in waste removes the unwanted by-products of excessive consumption away from the consumer and further alienates the consumer from the social and environmental impact of their actions. As a result the consumer is detached from the social and structural origins of their patterns of behavior. First, the manufacturing process of the product to be consumed is something the consumer is only vaguely aware of, and second the waste removal is also something that is not immediately obvious to the consumer. Such distanciation also disconnects the consumer from their social and environmental responsibilities.

As I have demonstrated elsewhere, the changing nature-society relations of late modern capitalism means that the awareness of dependence on ecosystems and on the natural environment for the survival of society has been lost with enlightenment philosophy and with the discourse of the mastery of nature (Kütting, 2000; Merchant, 1992). There are three counts on which the nature-society relationship is disturbed: changed rhythmicity through the imposition of mechanical onto ecological rhythms, Newtonian rationality based on studying parts rather than wholes, and disregard for the concept of entropy. All three counts can be found in the workings of the modern Western/ Northern consumer ethic and will be treated in more detail in the next section.

Although most of the problems associated with excessive and uneven consumption find their structural origins in the production process and in the social relations between state and firm, it is not possible to absolve the consumer from their responsibility in this process and therefore the consumer or consumption cannot be reduced to just being the last stage of production. Consumers are dependent on the supply chain in their choices of products and therefore constrained in their actions as they cannot themselves dictate supply except by indicating through their purchasing choices what is wanted. However, consumers are able to exert choices within a limited framework and they are also able to exert the choice of not consuming if it is not possible to consume ethically or in a more sustainable fashion. It is not convincing to take the consumer out of the equation by arguing that they are the unwitting victims of the production process or victims of the capitalist ethic of consumption. They are actors in their own right and as such vastly underresearched as a social, rather than marketing, phenomenon in global civil society.

CONSUMPTION AND EQUITY

This section will explore several ethical and/or equity aspects of consumption. First, it will look in more detail at the spirit behind modern consumerism and the underlying ethics of this approach. Then it will pursue a different ethical angle, namely the angle of unequal distribution of wealth in the global political economy and the consequences for consumption in that field.

Modern capitalism is accompanied by a fundamental mystery of consumption that goes beyond the natural human desire for more or new or better goods in the shape of 'keeping up with the Joneses.' As Campbell argues, 'the most characteristic feature of modern consumption is its insatiability' (1987: 37). Again, insatiability in itself is nothing new or extraordinary in historical terms but what is special about it in modern capitalism is that it is an insatiability across-the-board, a plethora of wants rather than a single-focus insatiability for one particular thing. Modern consumption is based on a tyranny of expectations, the expectation being that the material comfort of life will be qualitatively increased in a linear form, i.e., life will become materially better year after year. This linear expectation of progress and change for the better is a social by-product of the Enlightenment and creates what can only be termed a tyranny of expectations of life, not only in the consumption field but in general (Maniates, 2001). Society generally expects that its children have a better life, better jobs, better health, and better standard of living than the preceding generation. This is as good as considered an unspoken fundamental (Western) human right despite the fact that there is no logical or moral foundation for this assumption. Although some sections of society have taken a more post-materialist approach, notably the downsizers, the green movement, or certain religious groupings, the vast majority of the population in the North/West is deeply engaged in fulfilling insatiable wants as far as they can afford it.

In fact, the global economy is not only organized in order to achieve the cheapest/most efficient possible production process but also to guarantee the inflow of consumer goods to the consuming elite of the planet. Although neoliberalism pushes the policy of free trade, for example, the areas where trade liberalization has largely been achieved are those that benefit Northern/Western consumers such as capital goods. In the textiles sector, for example, where freer trade could lead to increased market access for developing countries, trade liberalization has not been forthcoming until very recently and the steps toward integrating textiles into the WTO framework have been hesitant and extremely gradual. This protects the Northern/Western industries. As many jobs have been lost in this fashion, there are strong fears in industrialized countries that further relocation of production facilities will occur. Hence, protective tendencies in non-liberalized sectors can be discerned. The issue of subsidies is another matter discussed in detail in chapter 6. However, non-globalizing industries' work forces in Northern states tend to be more em-powered than their Southern counterparts despite movements to the contrary. In fact, the structural basis of the current trade regime is geared toward supplying industrialized countries' markets to the most efficient and cheapest extent. Such policies can even be found in the policy advice given to appli-cants for structural adjustment policies as they are advised to grow cash crops that then leads to depressed prices for developed countries' consumers, if applied across-the-board.

CONCLUSION

The social and power relations underlying the structure of the global political economy are a very important subject that affects and are implicit in every sub-subject of this book. There is no question that there is a globalizing production economy in many (but not all) economic sectors but this is not matched by a global consumption economy. There is also no question that the global division of labor and global production aim to make production pro-cesses as cost-efficient as possible. This means that labor costs are kept as low as possible in many economic sectors and labor, health, and environmen-tal provisions are discouraged by the producers as far as possible in order to keep prices down. As a result global production benefits the producer by increasing profit margins but also consumers by making the product as com-petitive as possible. The breakdown of the Fordist model led to production being geared not toward a wider base of consumers (trying to open up new markets for new consumers) but toward the existing consumer base.

This means that post-Fordist forms of economic organization have had two consequences for the Northern/Western citizen. On the one hand, she has become part of economies of flexibility and the ensuing fundamental changes in labor relations. Any citizen in the world, if participating in the global economy, has to suffer the worries of job insecurity and as a Northerner/ Westerner having to take increasingly more responsibility for their own wel-fare in terms of pension or health provisions, etc.—or as a Southerner seeing the chances of such perks as far removed as ever. This is one side of the globalized world. On the other hand, though, the Western/Northern consumer who is the same person as the participant in the economy on the production side, has benefited in terms of steadily declining prices for consumer goods and for a wider choice of goods. Here, there is a fundamental difference in status between citizens in developing and developed countries. They share the insecurities and disadvantages of globalization but they most certainly do not share the benefits in terms of 'better' markets.

This argument in itself is nothing new and is intrinsic in many debates that focus primarily on production. However, a dimension of this problématique that has been the subject of much debate is the role of agency in this. Consumers are mostly portrayed as passive victims of the ever-evolving 'juggernaut' of modern capitalism who, because of their dependency on 'the system' for jobs and for survival and because of their natural propensity to want more, are the machinery that drives the economy either unwittingly or out of economic coercion. This is fundamentally a misleading picture and one that absolves the consumer of the 'sins' of the capitalist mode of distribution because the consumer is not seen in any role of active agency, nor as a 'holder' of structural power for that matter. In many ways this is true; however, consumers are aware of the fact that they can influence production processes through their purchasing power and boycotts and they have used this power successfully in the past. One only needs to remember the Brent Spar oil platform incident or South Africa. The power of the deviant consumer is as big as or, in my opinion, potentially bigger than the power of the resistance movements of global civil society that are generally seen as the 'saviors of the world in the face of corporate takeover' by global civil society researchers. It is true that consumer power remains a largely untapped power and a power that quickly subsides when media attention goes elsewhere because of its politically disorganized and non-institutionalized nature. Nevertheless, it is a potentially huge structural power. The point here is not so much consumer power per se but the issue of consumer responsibility. It is not sufficient to assign blame for an uneven distribution of wealth on the globe to the WTO, the IMF, the World Bank, or the multinational corporations without implicating the consumer as well. The consumer may not have the choice to opt out of the existing forms of social or economic organization but he/she has a choice in consuming or even not consuming and thus sending strong signals to the market. Ignoring this unused structural power is akin to the protester in Seattle in 1999 we all saw on our TV screens who trashed a McDonald's restaurant wearing a Nike sweater and sports shoes—it ignores structural linkages.

This becomes even more important in an environmental setting and when the issues of consumption and equity are highlighted. This theme will be continued in chapter 4 with a focus on equity and in the empirical section where consumption and equity become a key focus.

Chapter 4

Equity, Environment, and Global Political Economy

This chapter will explore some of the issues raised in chapters 1–3 and relate them to an equity dimension as the third pillar around which the argument in this book is organized. This is particularly pertinent with respect to the linking of environmental and social studies, as the analysis of environmental degradation is often carried out in the absence of any regard for the social and equity dimension. As global political economy is a topic intrinsically linked to equity and distribution issues, this topic is of prime importance both to environment and to wider global political economy (GPE) issues.

The connection between equity and environmental dimensions of international relations is rarely made as the environment in International Relations (IR) or in global political economy is generally treated from a strictly scientific perspective or as a purely regulatory matter (see, e.g., the regime literature). Thus, the environment is seen as a subject determined by cause-and-effect relationships and their effects on the running of international affairs need to be understood and managed. From this point of view seeing the environment as subordinate to the international system, it is as good as impossible to perceive of environmental values as such. However, there are many questions relating to the status of the environment and to how it relates to social status that are being addressed in other academic disciplines (Dobson, 1990; Little, 1999). This conceptualizing process also needs to be incorporated into IR or into global political economy.

There is no need to repeat the theoretical debates on ecocentric versus anthropocentric worldviews or deep versus shallow ecology in this context. However, some discussion needs to take place first of all on the intrinsic value of environmental resources and sinks but also on the distribution among global society of these resources and sinks as well as access to them. There can be no question that well-functioning ecosystems are needed for the survival of the human race and that therefore environmental protection in general is not a luxury but a necessity. Deforestation and desertification have a very real impact on livelihoods and also on global factors such as climate. Atmospheric problems such as global warming, ozone depletion, or acid rain are other examples of environmental degradation playing a major role for human survival but also for economic and political functioning. These problems and issues are generally agreed to have a significant social dimension and as such are important policy issues. However, the same cannot be said about, for example, species conservation as in the case of the tiger or the panda bear. These are not generally perceived to be vital issues. Although linkages in ecosystems are not well understood and therefore caution is advisable, it seems that these animals do not fulfill a role without which substantial damage leading to a threat for human survival might ensue. What role, then, should their conservation take? Is this a luxury or do we have a moral obligation to preserve species for future generations or do we even have an obligation to the species themselves? Should their preservation take precedence over the eradication of hunger or disease? Should it take precedence over the principle of state sovereignty, i.e., should states be allowed to 'interfere' in the internal affairs of another state when it comes to environmental conservation? What about the temporal dimension and intergenerational equity? These are questions that are not the direct focus of global political economy but nevertheless have a vital impact on our understanding of both political economy and environmental degradation. The first half of this chapter is dedicated to a more conceptual discussion of the terms of environmental ethics, equity, and justice and to how they relate to global society. The second half will link these concepts more explicitly to GPE and to the arguments of this book.

Critics of globalization argue vehemently that its processes lead to a downward spiral in terms of social justice and many of the arguments brought forward in this book so far support this claim. This argument is corroborated in this chapter and it is further argued that globalization also leads to a downward spiral in terms of environmental and not only social equity. Thus the second half of this chapter is dedicated almost exclusively to the issue and concept of social and environmental equity under globalization.

ENVIRONMENTAL ETHICS

The subject of environmental ethics can be neatly divided into two issue areas. The first is about the intrinsic value of nature/environment/ecology itself and how that relates to social relations. The second is about the value of nature/environment/ecology among societies both in spatial and temporal terms, i.e. a question of intra- and intergenerational equity.

The first issue to be discussed is the intrinsic value of ecosystems or the environment for society as such. Here, a distinction needs to be made between nature, environment, and ecosystems as these terms all have different meanings but are often used interchangeably in the social science literature dealing with the environment. In addition, all of these terms are highly value-laden, culturally specific, and socially constructed. Ronnie Lipschutz, for example, distinguishes between nature and Nature, the latter being a social construct (2001a: 72). To give another example, William Cronon's writings on wilderness serve as an effective illustration of this point:

> For many Americans, wilderness stands as the last remaining place where civilization, that all too human disease, has not fully infected the earth. . . .
>
> The more one knows of its own peculiar history, the more one realizes that wilderness is not quite what it seems. Far from being the one place on earth that stands apart from humanity, it is quite profoundly a human creation—indeed, the creation of very particular human cultures at very particular moments in human history. It is not a pristine sanctuary where the last remnant of an untouched, endangered but still transcendent nature can for at least a little while longer be encountered without the contaminating taint of civilization. Instead, it is a product of that civilization, and could hardly be contaminated by the very stuff of which it is made (1996: 69).

In common parlance, nature is usually referred to as something pristine or as something that has not been 'interfered with' by human or social practices. Given this definition, there is not a lot of nature left at the beginning of the twentieth century and using these strict definitions, 'nature' is more or less extinct. With global environmental degradation, there is arguably no area left that is unaffected by ozone depletion, global warming, atmospheric air pollution, marine pollution, or the existence of PCBs or endocrine disrupters. Penguins in Antarctica have chemical residues in their fatty tissues just as fish in deep oceans have been in contact with, and have been affected by, residues of oil pollution or ship paints. Thus strictly speaking nature is an obsolete term (although there are still wilderness areas) and is used more or less interchangeably with environment these days. Environment is a term whose etymology suggests the things that are 'around us.' Therefore it could refer to the built environment or the natural environment. Environment does not have to be pristine; it can be something that has been 'altered' by individuals or by society. So, a landscape that has been changed by agricultural patterns is part of the environment although it has not 'naturally' been transformed to this state. In fact, most environments today clearly have a human imprint on them ranging as far back as the early hunter and gatherer societies. Historically, different environments have existed in the same localities and therefore it is difficult to define a natural environment as environmental change is an important part of history. In addition, humans are not 'unnatural' and it is therefore difficult to draw the line where environmental change is seen as degrading and undesirable. The term ecosystem refers to the interplay between the various living organisms in a particular location and how they sustain life and the well-functioning of life-enhancing functions. Both ecosystems and the environment can be humanly altered as well as changed through other external influences. Neither environment nor ecosystems are static and it needs to be stressed that environmental change in itself is not a problem. There can even be 'natural' environmental degradation through volcanic eruptions or through naturally occurring forest fires, for example. These can lead to fundamental changes in ecosystems but they do not lead to permanent environmental degradation. Thus a distinction has to be made between environmental change and environmental degradation with the latter being of a more systemic and large-scale and irreversible nature than the former. This poses many definitional problems as Paul Little has argued:

> Ecological researchers must confront enormous methodological difficulties if they are to understand the historical conjunction of geological, biological and cultural temporalities, which have temporal scales that range from billions of years in the first case, to millions in the second, and thousands in the third. For example, the dynamics of frontier expansion in Ecuadorian Amazonia that involve oil development, colonization, deforestation, and conservation activities include at once the geological time frame of the formation of underground oil deposits, the biological time frame of the establishment of word-record levels of plant and animal diversity, and the cultural time frame of developmentalist frontier expansion, and have generated such responses as the depletion of oil deposits, reduction of biological diversity, and social stratification (1999: 262).

Thus the problem is not environmental change per se but rather the speed and nature of cultural change in recent times. Although environmental degradation is a condition that has afflicted all mass production, or capitalist, societies, massive global or time-space distanciated change has only happened with the rise of the fossil fuel economy. The economic tools used under modern capitalism and especially the production and financial patterns practiced under globalization have a large-scale systemic and often irreversible impact on the environment leading to probing questions on the ethics of such practices in environmental (and of course also social) terms. Under globalization the increasing time-space distanciation of rights and responsibilities for environmental degradation through the dependence on participation in the global political economy is unique. One example of this is the role of indigenous knowledge and use of indigenous plants for economic purposes:

> The rights to environmental knowledge developed and used by indigenous peoples and rural farmers have become a highly contested issue as a result of the growth of multinational biotechnology firms and their search for scientifically unknown, highly valuable plants, which has taken them to remote parts of the globe and placed them in contact with the local people. One response by local groups has been to issue calls for payment of royalties for use of their knowledge, and a more anthropological one has called into question the clash of cosmovisions whereby Western legal concepts of originality and innovation embedded in intellectual property law are not only sharply at odds with their indigenous counterparts, but are primed to serve the interests of biocolonialism (Little, 1999: 267).

Traditionally, governments have taken over the role of safeguarding natural resources, sinks, and protecting their citizens from environmental harm. Nationally this happens through the rule of law. Internationally, this has been effected through the role of international environmental agreements and through other more private forms of regulation. As governments are the appropriate legal channels through which such interests can be represented at the international level, there does not seem to be an ethical problem with this form of organization. However, under globalization there have been practical (but not de jure) changes in the role of governments at the international level. First, neoliberal practice suggests that market ideology and the market as a regulatory mechanism are the most efficient ways of dealing with social (including environmental) problems (Dryzek, 1987; Low & Gleeson, 1998). Thus governments have begun to participate in a division of labor resulting in a changing role. States now increasingly become the custodian of neoliberal ideology and push for well functioning markets. This has become their prime responsibility/task and it is assumed that the other tasks traditionally carried out will be adjusted through the market mechanism. Thus the traditional roles of the state have in many ways been transferred to private hands such as voluntary regulations but also many tasks have been out-sourced to private organizations, be they companies, research institutes, or civil society. It needs to be examined if there is an ethical problem with these dimensions as indeed Dryzek and also Low and Gleeson argue. At the least, there is a legitimacy and a temporal problem as out-sourcing or 'subcontracting' of traditional state roles do not guarantee their continued existence. Privatized responsibility is heavily dependent on continued support and funding and can more easily fall prey to discontinuation pressures than an established and acknowl-edged state responsibility.

One major ethical problem related to this is of course that the definition of what is in the public interest has changed. If the public interest gets narrowed down to issues of market efficiency, then clearly this has serious ethical but also equity repercussions. The shortcoming of liberal and neoliberal understandings of the public benefit are well known to be relative over abso-lute gains and it is generally acknowledged that this means that poverty gaps can and actually do widen. Implicitly, the ethical repercussions of this posi-tion have been accepted although this has not been publicly acknowledged. Given the dependence of society on a well-functioning environment for its survival, environmental protection is clearly an important issue and very much in the public interest. In many cases, it may interfere with other public inter-ests such as the eradication of poverty leading to increased consumption but it nevertheless is a high-priority issue on the public interest agenda. If the public interest is now defined in terms of market efficiency, then the public interest does not reflect the moral responsibilities of classical liberal democ-racy. This is predominantly a problem in the North as a geographical unit where such issues as the public interest have long been enshrined in political culture and are now being eroded. In other parts of the world where the concept of a public interest is not part of political culture or formulated differently, there is also an ethical problem in that there is not even a definition of public interest as such. The equity dimension of this will be discussed in the next section.

Another problem associated with this debate is the question of envi-ronmental ethics over time. When the ethics of environmental protection and access are discussed, they are often placed in a strictly contemporary and space-dependent context. However, all of these debates have a spatial and temporal component. The spatial component refers to effects across different societies and the temporal component refers to the impact that actions and behavior will have for future generations. Do we have moral responsibilities toward future generations or toward people in other parts of the world? General practice and humanitarian discourse seem to suggest that we have at least some moral duties toward people who are our contemporaries. This can be seen in the case of humanitarian intervention and humanitarian aid although this moral responsibility is not so acute when it comes to evening out structural inequalities or exploitative practices. However, in the case of intergenerational equity, the case is less clear-cut. Although international documents on human rights and international environmental treaties suggest that we do indeed have a duty toward future generations, this principle is more difficult to interpret and enforce. What would it entail—merely the clearing up of pollution or the actual preservation of resources for future societies? Although the principle has been enunciated in public discourse, there is no effective debate on this subject.

These points suggest that environmental ethics is a topic that has been neglected for two main reasons: on the one hand the culturally specific notion of what is ethical is problematic. On the other, the problem is the difficulty that 'the environment' cannot represent itself and demand to be treated ethically (and if it could, it would obviously not be one environment but many). These problems have been in existence throughout history and are not globalization-specific. However, under globalization and under the evolution of neoliberalism these problems have become more acute than ever.

ENVIRONMENTAL EQUITY

Unlike environmental ethics, the subject of environmental equity has a more anthropocentric focus. It is about control over, and access to, environmental resources and a clean living environment as well as distribution of resources. At the national level, research has shown quite clearly that it is especially people at the lower end of the social strata who are more exposed to environmental degradation and suffer from health and deprivation problems. The reason for this phenomenon is that socially marginalized people cannot afford to live in areas unaffected by pollution and often have to live near industrial estates with pollution problems (Economic and Social Research Council [ESRC] Global Environmental Change Programme Special Briefing No. 7). In addition, they are less able to overcome environmental restraints through the purchase of healthier goods or filtering devices. In many ways, these findings can be extrapolated to the global level.

Of the various types of environmental problems, the North's are typically associated with industrialization while those of the South are associated with the more immediate environment such as deforestation, desertification, and polluted drinking water. (Porter, Brown, & Chasek, 2001). Urban problems are associated with both North and South. Global problems are structural and affect both North and South, albeit in different ways. It is obvious that of the more immediate environmental problems affecting one's living environment more directly, there is definitely an income gap as the higher-income groups in any society are able to buy themselves access to a clean living environment. Therefore it is no accident that slums or lower-income housing are often situated in the more polluted parts of town or closer to industrial estates. This has an effect on health but also on access to environmental 'goods'. Therefore there can be no misunderstanding about a close connection between income and environmental quality of life. This is not a new argument, however, and does not need to be pursued further here.

Nevertheless, this argument can be extended to the international and the global in that wealthier states can increase their environmental quality by, for example, getting rid of their toxic waste or by out-sourcing certain dangerous practices (Clapp, 2001). Trade in waste is a reality and it is also well-known that capital flight occurs in areas where there are less stringent environmental regulations. Thus there is a definite issue of environmental equity as not all citizens of the world have access to the same environmental rights and these discrepancies are used for profit in the organization of the global political economy. Although some inequity can be found in the environmental conditions of different geographical locations in the world as they are obviously not the same, these are inequalities generated by the structural constraints of the global economic system. An inhabitant of a mountain village in the desolate ranges of the Bolivian Andes obviously has different food access than an inhabitant of the lower Pyrenees in France. This is not a question of environmental equity. However, both inhabitants' ability to be in control of their respective environment is a question of environmental equity.

Another equity issue is the evolution of a global division of labor and the equity dimensions associated with this process. In this global division of labor some regions have clearly been relegated to an agricultural role in the global economy while others have the role of cheap labor supplier. Through the intrinsic connections between the various parts of the global economy these roles are not of choice but are dictated by global pressures. Thus environmental access and equity in terms of consumer goods, availability, etc. are pre-programmed with no realistic way out of this equity deficit. Again, this is a structural constraint of the global political economy and one that has existed throughout history in various forms of colonialism. What is different today, however, is that through the privatization of control, the interest in the continued well-being of a particular agricultural area or other economic region is not part of the political setup any more. Once one region is depleted in environmental or social terms, another region will take its place. Colonial masters were interested in the continued profitability of their land. There is a fundamental difference between the two.

Thus, different levels at which environmental equity is a problem at the international/global level can be discerned. First, there is the agenda-setting power of the various states of the world when it comes to environmental degradation. Second, there is their position in the world economy. Third, there is the issue of purchasing power and consumption.

The agenda-setting power of various actors in the international system is a fundamental environmental equity issue and is also a structural issue. In the field of global governance, it is particularly obvious in the phrasing of the climate change debate (Harris, 2001). There is a rift between different countries that can be superficially described as a rift between developed and developing countries although this distinction is simplistic and does not take account of the various energy-producing roles and the way in which different states will be affected by global warming. However, it can be argued that the debate has been framed by developed countries, who want this issue to be treated as a contemporary and future problem. Many developing countries see climate change as a historical problem and want past emissions to be incorporated into possible emission reduction strategies. This idea is not something that is discussed seriously in the diplomatic channels used for progressing on climate change. However, at the same time developed countries are quite serious that future emissions should be taken into consideration. The debate is clearly framed in such a way that 'today' is the baseline from which discussions on equity start but anything that happened before today is not part of the debate. This seems to be an example of agenda-setting power as there clearly is a temporal dimension to the debate concerned with today and the future. As temporality is an issue, it does not seem logical that it is not applied in both directions, i.e., past and future. However, this would dramatically change the whole responsibility and commitment and power dimension of the negotiations. Therefore equity takes on a very subjective meaning determined by the social and power relations of the interplay between developed and developing countries. Although the climate change example is a particularly dramatic case, it is by no means atypical. Thus agenda-setting power is a major determinant in environmental equity relations.

Agenda-setting power is an indirect, structural type of power but equity concerns are by no means limited to structural power. Equity problems can also be found in direct power relations between North and South or between any social groupings. Although coercion by violent means is a relatively rare phenomenon in the international system given the number of actors in it, the number of violent conflicts with an environmental or resource dimension is rising (Diehl and Gleditsch, 2001). In addition, there is financial and political coercion, which is a historical phenomenon and has become especially obvious through colonialism and through modern forms of colonialism. Although politically most states are independent and sovereign, through their economic position in the global political economy, which is a direct consequence of historical social relations, they are not. Power can also be exercised by the refusal to participate in problem resolution exercises as the withdrawal of the United States from the climate change negotiations demonstrates. Furthermore, the exercise of direct power through global economic institutions determines the way in which environmental resources and sinks are used.

This point relates directly to the issue of consumption. Environmental degradation is not only a problem related to production but equally, if not more, to consumption. Thus a phrasing of the sustainable development debate or of common but differentiated responsibilities is focused on production but ignores the consumption side. If the consumption side of the global political economy was included in economic analysis of environmental degradation, a different picture of responsibility and duty would arise. The exclusion of the consumption argument thus seems to draw after itself serious equity repercussions that have been neglected in traditional accounts of globalization and environment or even in standard development discourse.

Thus it seems that environmental equity is a subject that needs to be more at the forefront of both environmental and global political economy discourses. It is highly relevant to policy discourses as well as to issues of environmental ethics as well as to social justice. It is also an issue that has been taken up by social movements that pursue the question of global inequality and inequity very seriously, often using vocabulary such as social and environmental justice. However, equity and justice are not interchangeable terms and thus a distinction needs to be made.

SOCIAL AND ECOLOGICAL JUSTICE

The main distinction in this context between equity and justice is that equity is only concerned with a small part of justice and is a more measurable term than justice. Equity is similar to fairness but fairness and justice are not the same. Justice is dependent on the legal or moral code in existence and therefore is more embedded in certain principles. Justice is a Western concept. Equity is also a Western ideological concept but as it is based on a more narrow definition, it is more easily applicable and better understood as a neutralized term of equal distribution of resources or rights. However, the social science literature in this field has tended to focus more on social and ecological justice rather than on equity and the arguments of this literature will be discussed in this chapter. However, equity is a preferable term as it can be more easily appropriated in a universal sense.

Justice is a concept firmly embedded in notions of law and politics. Thus it is a tangible as well as a conceptual tool. It is also a social construct and as such can be used to impose intrinsically cultural notions of justice on to other societies. Therefore a global or rather universal concept of justice is inherently fraught with difficulties, even more so than general notions of social and cultural justice. As Nicholas Low and Brendan Gleeson put it,

> Ultimately, political and environmental ethics must address this 'big picture' because so many ecological and social problems have a systemic or structural basis. We need political-ethical frameworks which can help humanity to address those threats which it faces collectively. Nevertheless, if the struggle for justice is a real world

process then we must make clear how abstract conceptions are connected with real world events. Threats to the environment, however
global, are manifested in specific places and local contexts. If society is to change to accommodate new conceptions of justice, it is
necessary to demonstrate in an immediate and concrete way why the
existing means of dealing with environmental conflicts are inadequate. Social change on the scale which may well be necessary for
global society to carry on the task of finding and delivering justice
in and to the environment is likely to proceed in a somewhat piece-
meal and incremental way (1998: 3).

Although the argument that environmental change or degradation is manifested in particular places rather than in a global abstract is absolutely true,
it can also be argued that manifestation and structural origin of the problem
very often do not come together on a spatial level. The origin and the actual
location of a problem may be far removed and this is a question of responsibility and agency and how these issues can be approached. It also leads to the
questions raised here that are concerned with particular notions of environment-
related justice. In order to decide on what is 'just' one needs to have an idea
of what intrinsic value nature and environment have to global society but also
to specific locales and whether it is necessary to have a universal concept of
the value of nature. Discussions of social and ecological justice echo many
of the arguments about anthropocentrism versus ecocentrism. Dimitris Stevis
summarizes this as follows:

Subscribing to ecocentric or environmental justice visions of nature
is both liberating and dangerous. Ecocentric visions are liberating
because they disrupt the imperial parameters of anthropocentrism;
they are dangerous because they can suggest that we are all equally
implicated in harming nature. Environmental justice visions are liberating in that they deliver us from scientistic and naturalistic views
of nature; they are dangerous because they can suggest that nature
is nothing but another distribution issue (2000: 63).

This fundamentally reflects divisions of what environment-related justice
entails and that it requires choices. For discourses or even policies on this
subject, it is therefore necessary to develop an environmental ethic on which
decisions of environmental, social, or ecological justice can then be based.
In a way such an ethic exists with the sustainable development framework
of rhetoric, literature, institutions and international agreements. However,
this ethic is part of neoliberal discourse and ideology and as such not a
coherent body of socio-political thought on environmental matters. As part

of neoliberal 'speak,' it has neither a coherent theory of the environment nor a consistent structural basis.

No political ideology as such contains an environmental component as an original part of the body of thought and environmental thought has been added to liberalism, socialism, conservatism, and other ideologies. As such, it has a very anthropocentric content since ecological or environmental thought did not evolve organically as part of the ideology. Thus, contents of environmental or ecological justice will be informed by a mainstream ideology. As concepts of social justice are traditionally located in socialist thought, the linkage of social and environmental justice usually takes places from an ecosocialist perspective. This means that concepts of social justice usually embedded in socialist or social-democratic principles are extended to include environmental justice in terms of equity and conditions of living. At the international level and in IR theory terms, concepts of social justice (or equity) can be found, for example, in the core-periphery analysis of world systems theory or in structural historical materialist accounts of the world. Including an environmental or ecological perspective within these approaches would typically include an analysis of access to, and property relations with, environmental resources and sinks.

Concepts of ecological justice coming from an ecocentric perspective can add to this conceptualization of justice. To quote Stevis again at length:

> The fact that ecological politics and ecological justice require choices is well understood by various ecocentrists. Nonetheless, some of them also imply that social choice will be minimized because something outside of us is involved, i.e. nature. Most environmental justice advocates. . . . do not deny the objective existence of nature. Nonetheless, many of them act as if taking nature into account complicates the distribution of justice, obscuring the possibility that the same causes are injurious to both nature and people. I believe that we ought to be critical of those ecocentrists and environmental justice advocates that do not make explicit the political economy/ecology that undergirds their social and natural choices. This is not a simple process, however, because it is not the case [that] the ecocentrists need only [to] bring in society or that environmental justice advocates need only [to] bring in nature.
>
> It stands to reason that questions of social and natural choices are apparent with respect to most environmental issues, whether we are referring to resource use, pollution, spatial planning, parks and other natural reserves or museums. The issue, therefore, is the kinds of choices we are confronted with when dealing with nature, as conventionally understood (2000: 65).

Thus there is an understanding of the potential dichotomy between social and environmental justice that can only be overcome by an enlightened understanding of environment-society relations. Any perspective that is too focused on society or too focused on nature/environment neglects the relations between the two. Thus, a clear understanding of justice, or equity, must be based on the connection and interdependence between environment and society, making a holistic analysis the framework for any concept of justice. Interdependence here also needs to be seen in the context of historical environmental change and how social change has invariably led to environmental change and that the two are now interconnected and some traditional 'environmental' activities are now carried out by social agents. An example of this would be managed forest fires to take the role of naturally occurring forest fires. Thus human intervention as such is not seen as undesirable but it needs to be carried out in an ecologically aware context. The remainder of this section will now be concerned with an analysis of how liberal thought and concepts of sustainable development incorporate this understanding of environment-society relations.

There is a long tradition of liberal thought in designing the international system and it is thus the hegemonic ideology that is gradually being complemented and even replaced by neoliberal thought. However, in the field of ethics and justice, liberal theories of democracy are still predominant as neoliberalism prefers to 'deal with' these issues through market mechanisms and thus does not have to say much on the matter.

There are many different types of liberalism and the one that is most appropriate in this context is cosmopolitan liberalism as this most effectively reflects the global parameters of the subject matter. This type of liberalism is not based on national thought and has a global worldview encompassing a concept of universal human rights. Cosmopolitan liberalism and its ideal theory address the topic of inequality very directly:

> Rawls' ideal theory still addresses human needs and global poverty along two different routes. The first is by the ideal conception of the society of peoples as consisting of well-ordered societies. This gives rise, according to Rawls, to duties and obligations of assistance to societies burdened by unfavorable conditions. So every society now burdened by unfavorable conditions should be raised to or assisted toward conditions that make a well-ordered society possible. Because of the ideal conception of the society of peoples as consisting of well-ordered societies there is no need for a liberal principle of distributive justice (Langhelle, 2000: 302).

According to this argument, the very notion that societies generate order within and among themselves means that some type of social contract and social responsibility toward each other exists. Without going into the analytical details of this train of thought, it is possible to see this way of thinking applied through principles such as humanitarian aid or development projects. However, this analytical perspective does not raise the question of the very structures giving rise to inequality and how these structures are kept in place through unequal power relations that are being exploited. Therefore there is no questioning of the underlying reasons for 'unfavorable' conditions for some societies. Thus this liberal principle is based on a rather shallow interpretation of justice, however well-meaning and responsible it looks. It does not want to tamper with existing social and property relations and leads to increased equality through the according of political rights without touching the economic structures that give rise to inequality in the first place. Thus it is a purely problem-solving approach.

Another way liberal thought deals with the issue of cosmopolitan or global justice is through the concept of basic human rights. John Rawls sees as basic human rights the rights to life and security, to personal property, to a basic rule of law, to a certain liberty of consciousness, to freedom of association, to the right to emigration and to a minimum amount of economic security in terms of access to food (Langhelle, 2000: 302).

> For (Charles) Beitz, a global session in the original position would lead to the acceptance of a resource redistribution principle that would give every society a fair chance to develop just political institutions and an economy capable of satisfying basic human needs. This principle would function as a global difference principle and provide resource-poor societies with the economic means necessary to support just social institutions and to protect human rights (Langhelle, 2000: 303).

Again, these concepts of universal human rights look tempting but leaving aside the issue of universal desirability, the question remains: How can these political and moral rights be enforced and implemented and how do they tie in with the global political economy? Being resource-poor due to geographical location is insignificant in terms of social and environmental justice and equity. In addition, these liberal concepts of human rights and justice do not tie in with the reality of environment-society relations. The main idea behind liberal thought is that social institutions are needed to deal with problems of justice and that help is needed in establishing these institutions and once every society has got them, global justice can be achieved. The assumption is that once political rights are realized, economic rights will follow by definition. However, the arguments put forward in this book suggest that this is clearly not the case. In addition, there is no conceptualization of the relationship between environment and society in this school of liberal thought and this is highly problematic. This point will be explored in more detail in the following section.

GLOBALIZATION AND EQUITY/SOCIAL JUSTICE

In the global political economy, equity and social justice as an issue can be found in the formation of what Mittelman calls the global division of labor and power. These are threads that have already been taken up in chapters 1 and 3 in this book and can be identified as the main structural and social forces behind globalization. Under neoliberal forms of labor and power organization, equity and social justice are not concepts that are explicitly included in the definition of the main principles of this ideology. Neoliberal institutions such as the World Bank or the International Monetary Fund (IMF) are committed to the alleviation of poverty and environmental degradation. However, there is an unspoken assumption that this can be done without structural change (I do not count structural adjustment policies as structural change). In fact, social justice and equity are quite deliberately not a major issue in neoliberal circles because of the importance of the competition angle. It could well be argued that an excessive pursuit of equity or social justice could be perceived as a hindrance to the balancing force of competition and thus the compatibility between these aims would be called into question.
As Mittelman put it:

> Hence the contradictory nature of globalization: It offers major benefits, including gains in productivity, technological advances, higher standards of living, more jobs, broader access to consumer products at lower cost, widespread dissemination of information and knowledge, reductions in poverty in some parts of the world, and a release from long-standing social hierarchies in many countries. Yet there is a price for integrating this global framework and adopting its practices. Expressed or tacit acceptance of being encompassed in globalization entails a lessening, or in some cases a negating, of the quantum of political control exercised by the encompassed, especially in the least powerful and poorest zones of the global political economy (2000: 5).

The least powerful and poorest zones of the global political economy that Mittelman refers to need not be geographical zones but can be economic sectors or social groups. They do not necessarily exist in separation from other social forms and often coexist in the same places. In essence, globalization works well for those who are in control of their destiny while it works less well for those who are not. Thus the reference to the global division of labor and power since the division of labor in itself is an important tool of power and very determinative of where state and non-state power lies in the global political economy. For example, in the apparel industry sector, the global division of labor and power is very obvious in that major players sit in the Triad countries (North America, Europe, Pacific Rim) where company management and consumption takes place while garment processing is subcontracted to cheap labor countries that have no control over the production process. Nascent indigenous industries in developing countries are hindered in their development by the quota system of the Multi Fiber Arrangement as the World Trade Organization (WTO) is only beginning to take on board gradual textile trade liberalization. Wage competition between developing countries is used as an efficiency gain for producers who rarely use the same textile factory for more than three months before moving on to the next subcontractor. Under these conditions, environmental and health and safety or labor rights would be serious impediments to competitiveness and thus to efficiency. Thus, there is a global division of labor with a flexible and constant flux in developing countries with a downward spiral in terms of wages and workers rights while the power over decisions and the power of ownership remains firmly in the Triad states with no transfer of power or capital and no 'globalizing' of power. Thus the relationship between the various state and company actors in the global political economy does not change. The gap between haves and have-nots is not closed and no upward move by the have-nots can be discerned. This situation is being reinforced and perpetuated by global economic institutions despite their rhetoric to the contrary. So, the globalizing of production in fact leads to a perpetuation of the equity deficit between rich and poor.

However, this fact in itself is not a phenomenon exclusively associated with globalization but with most forms of economic organization and can be found through various if not all phases of history. The exercise of power to one's own benefit is not limited to liberalism or neoliberalism but rather is endemic in all power-holders. Likewise, this equity deficit can be found at the local, national, regional, and international level and is thus a phenomenon both between and within societies. The reason why this phenomenon is problematic is not because these are unprecedented events but because globalization rhetoric is about freedom, global citizenship, and increased choice. This neglects to point out that this freedom and increased choice are available to an increasingly smaller segment of society (albeit the actual numbers of beneficiaries have increased in industrialized countries).

There is an analytical argument for the separation of economic and political rights. Clearly, under globalization processes and with the rise of the United Nations, progress has been made toward universal human rights. These may be based on liberal ideology and not reflect the cultural heritage of global citizenry but nevertheless they constitute an attempt at introducing a notion of equity and basic democracy. One should not forget that the notion of equity and social justice in itself is a Western concept arising out of liberal roots. These are political rights that are meant to apply to every individual on this planet but of course there is an implementation deficit and the implementation deficit in this context is not found at the national but at the global level. However, the basic assumption enshrined in the UN charter of human rights, which stipulates that all people are equal and have a right to be treated with dignity, whether actually implemented or not, has severe repercussions in the way equity concerns need to be weighted in the organization of the global political economy. This is where economic rights come in. Given the existence of these political rights, they also need to be reflected in economic reality and cannot be seen as non-applicable in this sphere. Thus an organization of the global political economy in which non-competitive elements are expected to drop out at the bottom and become non-participants in the game, can be seen as socially unjust and inequitable both in terms of a moral aspect but also in the face of the universal ethical code of conduct that the very same actors work by. So even by their own rules, there is an equity deficit although this is not acknowledged.

This equity and social justice deficit can be found in the policies of the World Bank, the IMF, the World Trade Organization, and even in the UN. The global division of labor and power overrules or arbitrarily applies the very same ethical or moral code of conduct stipulated by these institutions—it provides the structural base from which power is exercised. This is a fundamental, severe, and grave consequence of globalization and a fundamental intrinsic contradiction in the global neoliberal rhetoric. Rights are related to power and property; they are not something every individual is practically entitled to. It applies in the social field just as much as in the environmental field. This equity and justice deficit has been criticized by many actors and many social movements are deeply involved in a struggle to counteract this disenfranchising by global forces. The remainder of this section will now look at how concerns of social justice and equity have been taken up by various actors concerned with these transgressions.

GLOBALIZATION AND ENVIRONMENTAL EQUITY

As has been established in detail in this and in chapter 3, there is a serious environmental equity deficit in the process of globalization that goes hand in hand with environmental degradation per se. In fact, it could actually be argued that the root of environmental degradation is the existence of a lack of social justice and equity.

The perpetuation and active pursuit of an acceleration and worsening of this process by the major actors in the international system has led to the establishment of a resistance force that has taken up the cause of social justice in the social and environmental field. It pursues the aim of either fighting for social justice by fulfilling a reform role within the existing system or by sabotaging and disrupting the workings of the international system with protest movements that do not want to be co-opted into the policy process. These are reformist non-governmental organizations (NGOs) willing to cooperate with the powers that be in order to bring about change and the radical protest movements aiming to disrupt these policy processes respectively. Both strategies have had remarkable success in the near past and have attracted huge attention by the media, academia, and policy makers alike. Global civil society actors are now routinely part of the policy process and at the same time the 'unruly' protest element has been successful. Their success can be measured by the fact that there are major forces at play that try to undermine the potential power of these movements because of their disruptive power. Trying to avoid these protests have led policy makers to work hard on the margins of what is democratically 'legal' with new legislation on the right to assemble, E-mail surveillance, moving meeting to places where there is no legal right for mass public assembly, etc. In addition, the media attention these protests have received have seen backing by public opinion that has led to an erosion of perceived legitimacy of actors, most prominently the WTO.

Both global civil society strategies have had a political impact. However, it could be argued that this political impact has not led to an environmental impact. Although environmental groups are being consulted by the World Bank, this policy change has not really had time to 'bite'. Hence it is too early to come to any conclusion on whether global civil society involvement in policy-making will actually lead to structural changes in policy. Experience from social policy such as gender issues tends to suggest that the influence will be rather marginal. This may be related to the type of movement admitted to the negotiation table as there is a highly selective process. Many environmental organizations can be deeply conservative and not interested in structural change at all. In addition, other organizations such as the IMF or the World Trade Organization have not opened up (yet) to such participatory pressures—although the corridors of power are open for other non-state actors such as multinational corporations. This is clearly perceived of as a democratic deficit by the general public. On the other hand, the UN has a long history of NGO involvement but due to the nature of the international system this involvement is largely of a consultative nature and thus dependent on the goodwill of the main actors and related to issue areas. The number of NGOs involved in the Rio or Johannesburg summits or climate change negotiations may be impressive but their main influence is in the sphere of information production and dissemination.

There are several social justice and equity arguments associated with global civil society actors. Among the most important are the way in which these actors can bring social justice issues onto the global agenda but also whether these actors are legitimate agents in the international system and should be given a wider role. States are still the only sovereign actors in the international system and the only legal representatives in international organizations. Even the European Union (EU) as another legal actor is composed of states. Many international organizations and indeed many governments give NGOs official consultation status but this is as far as their legitimacy goes. Active input into policy processes is limited to information dissemination and no active participation in decision-making is on the cards. However, in terms of structural power rather than legal power or legal status, an NGO can play a substantial role in global governance. Research organizations such as the Institute of International Applied Systems Analysis in Vienna or the International Union for Conservation and Nature in Geneva are important organizations in determining the validity of scientific evidence or in shaping public or expert opinion. So, although an organization may not have the same legal status state actors have, they can exercise power and influence through other channels. Thus they can act as a source of expertise or as a public conscience.

In addition, there are many unofficial and voluntary regulation developments in the global political economy and NGOs play a major influence in this field. This is the privatization of global governance referred to earlier. Here, global civil society can play a much larger role. Lipschutz accounts for this with reference to the textile industry:

> Much of this action and activism has come to be focused not on politics, however, but on markets. By this I mean that a growing number of campaigns seeking global social regulation are utilizing consumer pressure on capital and 'corporate accountability' as a means of improving labor conditions in factories, reducing environmental externalities from industry, and controlling production and shipment of various kinds of goods in cross-border commodity chains. Many of these campaigns have been highly successful, but only up to a point (2001b: 5).

Social justice or equity issues are generally seen as legitimate concerns by public opinion in general and thus global civil society organizations are generally seen as 'the good guys'. However, this is not necessarily so and therefore the question of legitimacy continues to loom large as a major concern in global governance. First of all, there is a question of representation and office. Civil society actors have not been elected to represent a certain cause and although membership in an organization by large numbers of people does indeed accord a certain amount of legitimacy, this is uncertain territory. Likewise, a general viewing of civil society as 'the good guys' is also problematic as organizations representing patently undemocratic values such as racism are also civil society actors and may indeed have a sizable membership. In addition, many economic actors are also civil society actors and this is an issue of definition. Even if civil society is taken to mean 'social' actors and specifically excludes companies, it still includes employer federations or industry federations. Therefore there needs to be a yardstick by which the legitimacy of a cause can be measured and thus the legitimacy of the actor representing this cause. The only organization or actor who could indeed introduce such a yardstick must be a currently legitimate actor that leads us back to states and international organizations as the guardians of social justice, equity, and environmental values.

Thus the question of environmental ethics in globalization remains a difficult one and it can only be argued that there is an agency and legitimacy problem surrounding this issue. Global civil society adds the voice of the disillusioned and disenfranchised to the global political and corporate canon and this is an important voice but it cannot be listened to uncritically. However, it seems to be the only voice that actively speaks up for environmental and social equity as the main concern.

CONCLUSION

This chapter has explored the concepts of environmental ethics, equity, and social and ecological justice. Rather than putting forward a particular position on these issues or developing an environmental ethic, the problématique underlying the social construction of nature and the various constructions existing in different cultural and temporal settings have been touched upon. It has been argued that both concepts of equity and of social/environmental/ ecological justice arise out of a liberal framework but that they nevertheless have universal validity because they extend the same basic rights to all people and to ecosystems. In order to approach equity and social justice in an environmental context, structural conditions of the global political economy need to be studied and analyzed.

The global economy and economic theory in general in the twenty-first century is based on a concept of market forces and unlimited resources. Scarcity can be dealt with through market and price mechanisms but is not a 'real' problem, only a problem of supply regulation. For globalization and the environment this means that the supply of the global market is the most important task to be fulfilled and looking after the resources and sinks that make this supply chain possible has been externalized from the system. Thus, if a 'supplier' takes measures to prevent environmental degradation, conserve resources, etc. the extra cost of these activities leads to decreased efficiency and competitiveness and the 'supplier' thus makes themselves uneconomical. This is a serious environmental equity and social justice problem as it leads to the social and environmental degradation of those in the global division of labor who do not have choices to do otherwise. At the same time, the Northern consumer has increased consumption choice. This economic reality is in stark contradiction to the rhetoric of multilateral economic institutions such as the World Bank and the World Trade Organization that argue that increased market liberalization and efficiency will lead to the eradication of poverty and environmental degradation.

Part II

Eco-Holism in Practice

Chapter 5

The Political Economy of Garments,
Especially Cotton

In this section, the issues and concepts raised and discussed in chapters 1–4 will be reconsidered and looked at from a more empirical perspective. Cotton and garments have been selected as an illustrative case study because the garment industry is a globalizing industry to which all of the issues and concepts discussed previously pertain. They are both underresearched and at the same time some of the most socially and environmentally degrading industries in existence. This chapter will study the global political economy of cotton production and garment consumption from a historical perspective and trace the social and structural origins of degradation in a globalizing political economy.

The textile industry is one of the most important industries globally with over twenty million jobs depending on it both in developed and developing countries (Nunnenkamp, 1995). The cotton section of the textile industry still constitutes about 50 per cent of the world textile needs (Pesticides Trust, 1990; Dicken, 1992) although synthetics are catching up. As the major non-food crop, cotton is a major source of pesticide problems, especially in developing countries (Pesticides News, June 1995). In addition to the negative health and environmental effects of pesticides use, the development of insect pest resistance arising from the excessive and inappropriate use of pesticides is a serious threat to production in many countries (ibid.). Within cotton production, it is possible to identify the use of toxic substances from the agricultural production stage through to the final product. They affect the health of workers in all stages of production, lead to allergies in consumers, and degrade the environments of residents near cotton plantations. In spatial terms, there is local as well as global degradation through global production methods and consumption.

THE HISTORICAL SIGNIFICANCE OF COTTON AND TEXTILES

The history of cotton and textiles is inextricably linked to the history of modern capitalism. However, it is not the aim of this book to retrace this history of the rise of the British Empire on the back of the textile industry and all that it entails. Histories of these events can be found elsewhere (Dodge, 1984). Clothing and garments are a sign of civilization and all societies have been engaged in some form of garment production, be it weaving or the preparation of bear hides. In some cases, these endeavors may be called industries; in others they may have taken place at the household level. A dramatic rise in the production and consumption of garments took place after 1750 with the evolution of a fashion industry in the industrialized countries. During the same period, between 1760 and 1850, the amount of unprocessed cotton transformed in the British textile economy went up from 2 to 366 million pounds (Braudel, 1993: 382). The scope of this fashion and consumer society has increased steadily since, dramatically picking up in speed in the 1970s. However, this is not a global phenomenon. In many non-Western societies, fashions are longer lasting and the turnover rates of garments are also much slower as a consequence.

The historical linkages between different parts of the globe in terms of cotton and garment production and consumption will be discussed in this chapter with special reference to Africa in order to tie in with the contemporary illustrative case study of chapter 6. Although historically the social and environmental dimension of such analyses has been neglected, it will nevertheless be possible to at least ascertain their significance. To recap very briefly, with the rise of modern capitalism and the industrial revolution, countries such as Great Britain became major garment producers, not just in the wool but also in the cotton sector. As cotton does not grow in North Western Europe, the import of cotton was obviously a major determinant of global economic relations and an important policy issue:

> Manufacturers had no local supplies to draw on but had to reach thousands of kilometers away to secure steady supplies of cheap raw material to produce inexpensive commodities. By the mid-nineteenth century the vast amount of cotton circulating on the world market demonstrated the power of capitalist manufacturing to call forth the raw materials . . . [*that are*] required. But looking at the supply of cotton on the world market does not demonstrate the antagonistic and contradictory aspects of its development or how interdependent and heterogeneous were the systems of production and marketing throughout the world. French efforts to develop cotton in the West African colonies must be understood as part of world-wide engagement between globally structured markets, the expansion and periodic crises in capitalist production and dynamic local processes (R. Roberts, 1996: 6).

It transformed the economic landscapes in both developing and industrialized countries and encapsulated all the socio-economic changes of the period in a nutshell: colonialism, technological innovation, scientism, capital accumulation, and a new mode of production. It can also be seen as an argument for ecological world systems theory's explanation of the origins of environmental degradation. It shows that it is surely the mode of accumulation and mass production, rather than the mode of production per se, which is responsible for the degrading aspects of the political economy of cotton. The same goes for social degradation.

The relationship between core and periphery in the global political economy of cotton is illustrated well by Allen Isaacman and Richard Roberts:

> European efforts to promote African cotton production have a long history. It is a history that is intimately connected to the development and maturation of the world economy in the same period. Indeed, European interest in African cotton waxed and waned in direct relationship to the complex set of factors integral to the making of the world economy in the nineteenth and twentieth centuries, to the changing place of European nation states in that system, and to the changing political economies of European nation states. The cotton textile industry was a central consumer production sector in all of the European nations that scrambled to control African territories in the late nineteenth century. Not surprisingly, cotton held a primary place in European colonial agricultural policies throughout Africa ... European efforts to promote cotton production in Africa were linked to the development of industrial capitalism and to imperfections in the world supply of raw materials (1995: 1).

The tug and pull in the social relations of colonial cotton production are a clear reflection of the market supply interests of colonizers and guarding of self-interest by the colonized's peasantry. Technological innovation in the textile processing sector led to Britain ousting India from the largest cloth/garment producer position by 1780 that in turn led to vastly increased demand for the raw material cotton. This was largely fulfilled by the burgeoning American market but the American Civil War and the boll weavil plague in the late nineteenth/early twentieth centuries showed the necessity for other markets. Africa had a long history of cotton production and an image of tropical abundance ideal for cotton production. Hence there was a strong interest by the colonial powers to expand cotton production in Africa and they undertook moves in this direction.

For African peasants and local merchants however, the infrastructural changes undertaken to promote cotton production were often used for other purposes. Preference was given to other crops such as groundnuts that brought the peasant a higher rate of return. There was also an issue of food security as this 1941 report in a Mozambican newspaper shows:

> The expansion of cotton production . . . and of other forced cultures have had a prejudicial effect on corn and peanuts which are indispensable to the Africans' diet and no less profitable to the producers than cotton. It is excellent, even magnificent that cotton production has increased . . . but it does not make sense for the colonial economy that this expansion should come at the expense of corn (Noticias, 19.7.1941 in Isaacman, 1996: 159).

Isaacman continues:

> In a confidential report to the president of the Cotton Board six years later, a senior agronomist concluded that 'it is becoming increasingly more appropriate to attribute food shortages to cotton'. The situation had not improved by 1950 when the bishop of Beira expressed outrage that in one of his parishes which had been a rich granary producing an abundance of food . . . the introduction of cotton had left the people living in the region suffering from hunger (1996: 159).

In some cases food production was interrupted through the destruction of crops and through the forceful introduction of cotton crops. In general, colonialists tried to promote cotton growing through the removal of local layers of bureaucracy and a guaranteed maximum price. Despite these efforts African cotton still found it difficult to be competitive on the world market as U.S. cotton was easier to process and the United States had a more sophisticated and cheaper transport system for bringing the cotton to the textile mills. In addition, excessive cotton growing in African areas often led not only to food shortages but also to environmental problems as laborers were forced to work the plantations that led to soil and labor shortages for food-based agriculture. So, overall historically the use of large-scale cotton production in Africa is an outside-driven process. Although there has always been a domestic cotton industry, this was geared toward satisfying local demand and thus operated on a much smaller scale.

To relate this back to the history of the global political cotton economy, colonial attempts to establish an African supply network of cotton were only partially successful and other world regions became more prominent cotton producers. After 1945, officials realized that for cotton production to be successful, prices had to be competitive for farmers and cotton needed to fetch as good or better a price as other crops (Isaacman & Roberts, 1995: 11). In response to this wisdom and to the numerous food crises, Africa tended to produce largely for regional consumption up to the mid-1990s. The largest post-war cotton producers are the United States and many Asian countries.

The historical context of cotton production shows that with the rise of colonialism and the ensuing social relations, technological innovation and increases in world trade were evermore directed at ensuring the maximum supply and efficiency at minimum price for the colonizing countries. Thus cotton and colonialism are intrinsically linked in the African experience. However, the use of African land for European cotton mill supplies was not an unproblematic one as these experiences show. Although African farmers were bound into global production and power structures, their ways of resistance to the cotton regime were manifold and influenced colonial cotton policy. The modern situation of cotton as a cash crop to pay off debt can in many ways be compared to the colonial situation in terms of global production and power structures. The fact that cotton has emerged as a major cash crop in West Africa is an undeniable consequence of the colonial experience.

COTTON AND TEXTILES TODAY—
FROM PRODUCTION TO CONSUMPTION

Production

Today, cotton is grown in over eighty countries under a variety of social and geographical conditions (UNCTAD, 1996). The five largest cotton producers are China, the United States, India, Pakistan, and the Commonwealth of Independent States (CIS) while the biggest per capita garment consumers are located in the United States, Switzerland, and Germany. Although the United States is the world's second largest cotton producer, the majority of cotton growers are located in developing countries. Ownership patterns range from large corporate plantations to small-scale farming. The textile industry is one of the most important industries globally with fifteen million jobs depending on it both in developed and developing countries, as well as a further eight million in the clothing sector (Dicken, 1992: 234). The cotton sector of the textile industry still constitutes about 50 percent of the world textile needs although synthetics are catching up fast (Pesticides Trust, 1990). This trend is fashion-dependent and cyclical.

Only about one third of cotton fiber produced finds its way onto the international market and the rest is consumed domestically (UNCTAD, 1996). However, even if a country's share of the world cotton market is small in percentage terms, this share may still constitute a large amount of their export earnings. For example, cotton is the most important export earner for African countries such as Chad, Burkina Faso, Benin, and Mali constituting more than 40 percent of their export earnings while contributing less than 5 percent to the global total cotton production share (Financial Times, January 30, 2002: 9). Some states such as China and Pakistan tend to export cotton in processed and manufactured form rather than cotton fiber. That makes it difficult to determine the export share of global cotton production. This also means that the global cotton chain is subject to varying practices and that it is difficult to generalize production patterns.

The last few decades have seen drastic changes in production methods and trade in this sector and the rise of developing countries as major producers. However, world trade is still dominated by developed states' output (Dicken, 1992: 239). Cotton crops are bought by cotton commodity traders who operate in a largely oligarchic market (Clairmonte & Cavanagh, 1981; Dicken, 1992). These cotton commodity traders sell the raw material cotton to the textile industry. The next link in the textile chain is the processing of the cotton into yarn and then cloth. A variety of large and small companies operate in these businesses. A large, concentrated market exists at the end of the textile chain, when the textiles become garments (although only about 50 percent of textiles are processed into garments) (Dicken, 1992: 234). The largest share of the cotton crop ends up in the developed world's shopping malls (in the US) and High Streets (in Europe), which are dominated by relatively few large retailers in most countries.

World Bank and International Monetary Fund (IMF) policies encourage the growing of cash crops for the world markets in order to alleviate the problems of the debt crisis in developing countries. This is also the case in West Africa. At the same time, there is resistance to opening up markets for textiles. As Taring Banuri argues:

> Because of shifting comparative advantage, there has been a rapid expansion of the textile industry in the South, especially among cotton growing countries. Textile production has traditionally been the first industrial sector of many developing countries and has paved the way for broad scale industrialization and economic expansion.

> [A] stylized fact of the market for cotton and cotton products is the existence of special trade barriers against southern industrial products. Textiles are a labor-intensive industry and provide a comparative advantage to southern producers. However, the shift of the industry to the south has been slowed down, and the interests of traditional northern manufacturers protected under various unilateral, bilateral and multilateral agreements (1998: 7).

I will further emphasize this point by outlining the existing political framework for the trade aspects of the global cotton chain. This global production process is currently regulated by the Multi-Fiber Arrangement (MFA) which is in the process of being phased out. Textile trade is slowly being incorporated into the General Agreement on Tariffs and Trade/World Trade Organization (GATT/WTO) framework. However, this type of international regulation is solely concerned with barriers to trade and tariffs and quotas. There are a multitude of studies of the MFA and power relations concerning the textile trade (Schott, 1990; Yang, 1994; Hale, 2002). It is particularly noteworthy that the textile industry has until recently been excluded from the trade liberalization moves of the post-war period and is one of the most heavily regulated trade areas that imposes hefty trade restrictions on developing countries. The studies on trade regulation through the MFA provide insightful analyses of the trade aspect of the textile industry and on the discourse of free trade in general but they ignore the environmental as well as the social aspects relating to the global political textile economy. Graham Harrison (2001) summarizes the situation by showing that the IMF and the World Bank effectively make economic policy in Africa in general, thus also influencing cash crop policy decisions. However, textile issues are of minor relevance to West Africa as the textile industry does not play an important role in most countries' export figures despite many tariff exemptions (Mshomba, 2000).

In the absence of international regulation, attempts to mobilize against the problems in the cotton chain have largely been initiated by civil society. These efforts have so far largely focused on introducing codes of conduct for social rather than environmental standards. The large retailers have been singled out for cooperation by the social movements. It has not been investigated yet how interested the clothing multinationals are in introducing environmental standards or codes of conduct in the garment sector and how fruitful an approach based on voluntary code of conducts might be. This point is also relevant with regard to the increased share of genetically modified (GM) cotton. However, the focus of the new social movements on clothing multinationals shows quite clearly that there are strong linkages between the local and the global and that some locals have more influence over the global than others. It also shows that the focus is on production and that the role of consumption in this economic activity tends to be marginalized.

Consumption

As discussed earlier, the origins of the consumer society can be traced back to the industrial revolution and it is generally agreed that the first consumer society had emerged by 1800 (Campbell, 1987: 6). According to Neil McKendrick, the speed with which fashion changed increased quite remarkably between 1750 and 1800 (1982: 56) and Campbell argues that "The emergence of the modern fashion pattern is thus the crucial ingredient in any explanation of why either emulation on the part of consumers or manipulation on the part of producers should have begun to take such novel and dynamic forms in the eighteenth century" (1987: 22). Consumption is thus culturally as well as economically informed as the idea of a consumer ethic suggests and the cultural/social side has been underrepresented in political economy accounts. Mike Featherstone (1991) distinguishes between three main perspectives on consumer culture. First, consumer culture has developed alongside the expansion of capitalist commodity production that has provided the opportunity for accumulating vast amounts of consumer goods and has made this hoarding desirable. Second, consumption is used as a way of asserting social bonds or distinctions, or affirming or transcending one's class status. Third, the emotional pleasures of consumption and the concept of aestheticism associated with it have a powerful hold on industrial society, or even on what can loosely be termed human nature. The latter two points can also be seen in conjunction with the ever-rising importance of symbols in the legitimation of social organization (Sulkunen, 1997: 10).

When these three perspectives are applied to the consumption of textiles, or specifically to garments in the fashion industry, it can be observed how the concept of consumption has changed over time. Even as recently as the 1950s, consumers in Northern industrialized states usually possessed only one good suit/dress that was supposed to last for many years and was not subjected to the fierce fashion dictate known in the 1990s and early twenty-first century. One reason for increasing consumption is the steadily declining price of clothing that obviously provides the opportunity for consuming more. Even between 1987 and 1997 the price of clothing fell quite dramatically so there is a steady downward trend. Second, clothes are not just something we put on to keep warm or to express our feelings for a certain social occasion; they make a statement about our values and our class status or the class status we aspire to. Clothes have become not only image statements but primary indicators of a person's personality. Third, the ever-changing fashions require that our wardrobes are updated continuously to fit in with what is required aesthetically in order to be taken seriously in our professional or social fields.

Naomi Klein takes this argument even further in her book about branding:

> The scaling-up of the logo's role has been so dramatic that it has become a change in substance. Over the past decade and a half, logos have grown so dominant that they have essentially transformed the clothing on which they appear into empty carriers for the brands they represent. The metaphorical alligator, in other words, has risen up and swallowed the literal shirt.

... Advertising and sponsorship have always been about using imagery to equate products with positive cultural or social experiences. What makes nineties-style branding different is that it increasingly seeks to take these associations out of the representational realm and make them a lived reality (2000: 28–29).

Thus fashion, and clothing as a substantial part of it, has a profound impact on the consumption patterns of the consuming elites. This fashion revolution starting in the 1960s has affected both producers and consumers by fundamentally changing consumers' attitudes toward the volume and type of clothes they wear throughout the year and by exponentially increasing the demand for natural and synthetic fibers. Fashion is described as a post-Fordist industry (S. Miles, 1998: 94) which is highly flexible and responsive to consumer demand. Thus, fashion is seen as consumer rather than producer driven, supposedly giving the consumer more input into a previously producer-dominated product chain. This is not always the case however. Although certain logos fall from grace rather suddenly and are thus dependent on the consumer's whims, the political economy of fashion in many ways effectively steers demand through advertising, through use of media, and through personality cults around movie stars or other fashion icons determining consumption output. This leads to questions about power relations in the fashion industry. First of all, power in the fashion industry is concentrated in the hands of relatively few large retailers who have effectively ousted or radically reduced the market share of smaller manufacturers (S. Miles, 1998: 95). Second, as Miles, argues,

In effect, the fashion industry is not as flexible as it might seem on the surface. It would be naive to contest the idea that changes have taken place in the economy. Common sense tells us that there are more products on the market. But there could equally be an argument for suggesting that such choice is largely illusory. There may well be hundreds of different versions of the classic pair of jeans but essentially each of those jeans offers the consumer the same thing. The choice that is available is not only unnecessary but barely constitutes a choice in the first place because it so often amounts to little more than a very slight variation on a mass produced theme. In effect, consumer choice in the realm of fashion is inherently artificial (1998: 95).

Third, and intrinsically related to point two, choice for the consumer is inherently limited to choice within a particular fashion paradigm, i.e., what products are considered to be in vogue in any particular season. A consumer will find it impossible to purchase a garment that does not conform to the standards of what is considered fashionable during that season. Therefore consumers may have increased choice and influence on the production process but this choice only exists within certain clearly delineated boundaries—the premise on which neoliberal ideology is based. Effective advertising and the social standing of appropriate clothing intrinsically link the participation in the fashion dictate to social success, thus giving enormous social and economic power to the multinational clothing retailers. So, rather than consumers dictating to the fashion industry, the momentum works actually the other way around. Consumer power lies in the choice not to buy or to buy selectively. Occasionally it happens that the consumer eschews certain fashions and the producer or retailer is not able to sell them. So the consumer's influence on the production process lies mainly in the ability to reject what is offered rather than to influence production in the first place although, of course, rejection of certain types of fashion will lead to the producers taking these rejections into consideration for the next season. In addition, a large part of clothing fashion production is based on the just-in-time method that means that consumers can respond even in the same season. Still, it is also clear that consumer power is potentially enormous as argued before but in practice is not being harnessed. Given the substantial advertising budgets that have to persuade consumers to keep up their consumption habits, it becomes clear that the structural power of consumption is being suppressed.

The emerging spiraling pattern of consumption draws after it spiraling production to feed the demands of consumption (but with the producers more or less guiding what is being consumed). This is where the environmental angle on consumption is particularly important. Again, the consumer is removed or alienated from the production process and also from the disposal process of the clothes consumed. Most consumers are unaware of the dramatic social and environmental consequences of the production process of their clothes but also do not respond dramatically when certain malpractices are highlighted. However, although environmental degradation can be found in the production process, it would be limiting to find the solutions to this form of environmental degradation solely in the production process.

The demand for cotton in industrialized countries increased exponentially from the 1960s onward when the increased wages of the Fordist mode of production coupled with a changing set of values putting fashion or trendiness above quality led to a huge increase in clothing consumption both in Europe and North America. The majority of the population has subjected, and continues to subject itself to, an increasing degree to this fashion dictate. This has obviously led to vastly increased consumption that then impacts back on developing countries through vastly increased demand for raw materials but also in the form of cheap labor for the manufacturing of these clothes. The annual average new garment consumption in Europe is around 10 kg (22 pounds) and whatever discussions there are on the environmental consequences of textile production, they rarely focus on consumption. There are debates on the comparative sustainability of natural versus synthetic fibers, the viability of organic cotton, the possibility of hemp as a major fabric, etc. but the volume and nature of consumption is not a part of this discourse. Only the German NGO (non-governmental organization) BUND (Bund für Natur- und Umweltschutz Deutschland) has raised the issue of consumption in its debate on the textile sector. Thus it seems that it is not the actual volume of production that is being questioned by globalization critics but rather the nature of production. In addition, the problem is constructed in terms of a problem with economic organization that has to be solved at the macrolevel alone. The role of consumption and the 'collusion' of the consumer in all this is a subject that tends to be ignored by both policy makers (for obvious reasons) and by civil society.

The existence of sweatshops as a sign of the globalization era and the role of clothing multinationals has been the focus of many campaigns, press campaigns, TV documentaries, and consumer boycotts. However, the nature of the fashion economy is not an issue in these reports or campaigns. Rather, the analytical framework of the problem remains restricted to the relationship between manufacturer and sweatshop worker, the call for the recognition of labor unions, and the abolition of debt for developing countries so that they can introduce a fairer wage policy. These debates are surely timely and address important issues; however, they neglect the nature of the system itself.

There is also a social and cultural dimension to this argument. Fashion is not only determined by the industrialized countries; this social and cultural dominance is further reinforced (a) by spreading this fashion globally through cultural leadership and hand-me-downs and (b) by perpetuating the position of the 'poor relative' recipient. To explain this further, there are usually two types of fashion or dress styles in many developing countries, Western and local dress. Through the destruction or competition for local industries and the relative price competitiveness and popularity of the second-hand clothing market, a market for Western goods is created and the local product undermined (Hansen, 1999). This is globalization in a different sense as the one put forward by the cultural globalization writers as the structural origins of cultural homogenization are not a move toward a global village but rather toward the economics of the political economy of textiles.

Furthermore, this second-hand clothing market symbolizes the relative positions of the developed and developing world in the global political economy. The developing countries supply raw materials and cheap labor for assembly; the developed countries consume at low prices and then dispose of the garments in order to buy more products at cheap prices in the latest fashion. The disposed garments are then used either by the lowest income groups in developed nations or back in developing countries where the second-hand clothing market undermines local industries that would be a step on the way out of the dependent position of developing countries in the world economy. Thus the cycle is closed and the relative positions in the world economy reinforced.

The textile and garment sector is one of the most obvious economic sectors for observing the trend of Western consumption and Southern production. The main reason for this is the importance of fashion and fashion as a primary vehicle of advanced capitalism. This is one dimension of capitalism that is underresearched and neglected, mainly because most research in this field is either economic determinist or culturally determinist but rarely takes account of both.

One extreme illustration of this point is the culture of branding as described in detail in Naomi Klein's *No logo* (2000). Branding is an advertising gimmick that leads to more conspicuous consumption and to the determination of one's personality through the brands one consumes. Brands become lifestyles. The most famous examples of this type of branding are the cases of Nike and the Gap that have been widely quoted. However, branding goes through all layers of society and is not just a middle class phenomenon. Even ethical consumption often takes place through branded products, here Patagonia replaces Nike, or Ecover replaces Lever Sunlicht. Branding also absolves the consumer from the necessity to think. Once the consumer has chosen what sort of image they would like to project, they only need to shop in the right places. Thus slowly the consumer is alienated from the ability to think and judge for themselves about what constitutes good taste and/or common sense. By projecting and selling an image, a brand can now create all sorts of behavioral norms. For example, the ever-increasing turnaround of fashions and the need to keep up with them as well as the increasing lack of quality of garments are phenomena that are not questioned by consumers and are fully accepted as entirely normal and even desirable. Although these are producer-led trends, they need the full cooperation of the consumer in order to carry off trends such as branding or fashion. These trends play on the insecurities of human beings to be an acceptable member of their chosen group, to fit in while still being individualistic and competitive, and they also buy heavily into the beauty myth, selling an image of beauty that again is fashion dependent and that demands an aestheticism in a beauty-addicted society. Thus the consumer is an integral part of the machinery of garment production as one of the main beauty and style industries. Many social movements have realized the potential of consumer power and the intrinsic complicitness of the consumer in the practices of the global political economy. They have called for more openness about the production processes and more input into the policy-making processes. However, they have rarely called into question the nature of consumption per se unless they come from an environmental perspective. Even church groups have neglected to highlight the relationship between Northern consumption and Southern production in ethical terms. Rather, most civil society involvement in this field has concentrated on the conditions of production in developing countries in the textile sector.

THE SOCIAL SIDE OF PRODUCTION

The social and working conditions of textile and garment manufacturing in developing countries, particularly in the economic exporting zones (EEZs) in South East Asia have often been described as one of the most visible signs of globalization. They are also seen by many as a sign of economic takeoff as the sweatshops of nineteenth-century Britain are inextricably linked with the rise of capitalism. Therefore, the argument goes, the reproduction of these conditions in developing countries means 'going through stages' on the linear path to development. Such an argument is of course erroneous as it is based on the assumption that conditions for takeoff now and in the nineteenth century were the same and that Britain then and the developing countries now were in comparable situations economically, politically, and socially. Britain was not in the world's periphery when it underwent the industrial revolution unlike the developing countries today. Furthermore, it is based on a linear view of time in which development will come to all once they have gone through the right stages or jumped through the right hoops.

This section will highlight and put into perspective the social conditions of garment manufacturing. In the past twenty years profound changes have taken place in the geographical location of garment production. It has often been said that garment production has shifted from the developed to the developing world as an aspect of the post-Fordist mode of production. This is not entirely accurate. Industrialized states are still garment producers; however, their efforts are concentrated at niche markets or at the upper end of the garment market. For example, designer products or high-quality merchandise or specialist products are still produced in industrialized countries. However, the lower end of the market and a lot of high-fashion items depending on just-in-time manufacturing have indeed been out-sourced to developing countries and it is here that scandalous working conditions have often grabbed the headline news (CAFOD, 1998).

There are several aspects to this kind of production practice. First of all, there are the actual working conditions. Workers often have to work at a minimum wage that is not a living wage. As production takes place in low-wage countries whose main advantage in the global labor market is exactly the low-wage economy, this competitive advantage has to be exploited to the fullest extent possible. If the wage structure gets revised, other countries may offer cheaper labor and the employment opportunity may go another way (CAFOD, 1998). This has often happened and therefore the interplay between state, company, and worker is a difficult and fraught one. The developing state has to argue that low-wage labor is better than no work at all for its citizens and furthermore that the usual local wage is usually no higher than the one offered by the international textile company. The worker cannot survive on the wages offered but without these jobs, the situation would be even worse. The winner all-round is the company that gets its products manufactured with the cheapest labor cost. It can play off one state against the next in getting the best deal. However, some writers argue that there is no empirical evidence for the lowering of labor standards and that conditions have actually improved under globalization (Drezner, 2001: 66). This may be true but certainly the existence of below living wage standards have been used to advantage in the global economy at the expense of jobs that were paying living wages or that were subject to labor standards.

Another point of grievance is the conditions under which textile production takes place. The term sweatshop conjuring up conditions from another era is used to describe what is going on in garment factories, particularly in South East Asia and in Latin America but often also in industrialized states such as the United States or the United Kingdom. In particular, forced overtime, no breaks, child labor, and inhumane work environments with no windows and no ventilation are the main issues. These conditions have been documented elsewhere in much detail; suffice to give one example of another aspect that has not received so much attention. Kitty Krupat in Andrew Ross's *no sweat* describes a monitoring visit to a textile factory in Honduras:

> August 1995, San Pedro Suala, Honduras—At 6.30 a.m. workers arrive at the gate of Orion Apparel, a Korean-owned factory in San Pedro Suala that produces Gitano shirts and sportswear for other American manufacturers. Each worker is searched as she goes through the door. Standing in line with them are Charles Kernaghan and Barbara Briggs of the National Labor Committee Education Fund in Support of Worker and Human Rights in Central America. Dressed as American business executives, they walk through the door unquestioned. With them is a camera crew, filming the line as it passes into the factory. Once inside, Kernaghan and Briggs begin asking questions: How old are the workers? What do they earn? How are they treated? One fifteen-year-old tells them she works till 8.30 most nights. She is the sole support of eight people in her family. She earns 38 cents an hour. The same girl tells Briggs that supervisors

yell at the girls and hit them. Another says workers are forced to take birth-control pills in the presence of plant supervisors. . . . That night, Kernaghan, Briggs and their camera crew are escorted to a factory garbage dump by Lesly Rodriquez, a fourteen-year-old Orion worker. The camera surveys piles of garbage, zooming in on hundreds of aluminium packets that once contained birth-control pills (1997: 51).

This report by a (U.S.) National Labor Committee official also describes problems that have not received as much attention such as physical abuse.

The vast majority of garment workers are women and often young girls. In some countries they tend to be married women but in many countries they are girls sold or forced into the apparel industry as an alternative to prostitution. This type of work can only be done for a few years before the body is worn out and the women are then often seen as outcasts by their own societies. At the same time, their families are dependent on the income the garment factory work raises for them, inadequate as the pay may be. Because of the social position of the garment workers, sexual intimidation and harassment can be carried out without punishment.

The response to these catastrophic conditions in the apparel sector has of course been collective organization through unionization. However, many factories have outlawed unions in order to keep up Victorian conditions. Here the fear goes in two directions. On the one hand, they fear the demands of a collectivized work force and the cut in profits a work force with labor rights will lead to. On the other hand, a collectivized work force cannot remain competitive at the international level and in such a fast-moving environment, a loss of profitability and price competitiveness will more than likely lead to the closure of the factory and thus to the loss of the jobs involved.

This point is not just an idle threat of factory owners. Production mostly takes place in economic export processing zones that are exempt from international import and export restrictions. These zones are incentive areas for attracting foreign investment and are thus highly competitive. In fact, in the garment industry, production facilities used by the large multinationals usually change every three months or so, always in search of the cheapest labor force.

The international and global aspects of the organization of garment production shows quite clearly that international solutions are required for these problems. National legislation is not really an answer as the political economy of textiles is currently structured in such a way as to play off the needs for foreign investment by the various developing countries involved in garment production. Therefore there is a race to the bottom in terms of low wages, workers' rights, and environment regulations as these interfere with price competitiveness.

This is a problem that has been recognized more by industrialized states than by developing ones. In the true spirit of 'it is better to be exploited than not to be exploited at all' the exploitation of work forces are not a primary concern of developing countries' governments as they know that without this their work force may well be unemployed that would be even worse. Thus the resistance at Seattle in 1999 during the infamous WTO ministerial round by developing countries to global labor and environmental standards has to be seen in this light. Global standards would take away their competitive advantage in terms of offering the cheapest (and by implication most exploited) labor.

So, ironically there is a tacit alliance between clothing manufacturers exploiting the competition for garment production facilities and developing countries suffering from the abuse of the situation but still being dependent on this type of investment. This makes the tackling of these problems particularly difficult and it also raises questions of agency and legitimacy. Since many developing countries are clearly against global standards, who will then speak out for the exploited labor force's plight? And furthermore, those actors that have taken on this cause such as NGOs and even some consumers work very hard to improve the situation through corporate responsibility awakening, etc. However, questions remain as to whether they are legitimate actors and how qualified they are to speak on behalf of the garment work force.

THE ENVIRONMENTAL SIDE OF
PRODUCTION AND ITS REGULATIONS

Continuing the list of problems in the political economy of textiles, this section looks at the international/global political economy of textiles in relation to the environment. This includes a discussion of international efforts to regulate environmental problems relating to textile production.

In terms of cotton agriculture, the intensification of agricultural production methods has resulted in a worldwide increase in pesticide use. There are several adverse effects of pesticides on humans and on the environment: Excessive or inappropriate use leads to pesticide poisoning with severe health effects such as allergies, liver, and kidney damage; cancer; or male sterility. Local pesticide residues affect air and water quality. Due to their mobility in air and water, they also affect ecosystems far removed as well as people. The existence of pesticides in breastfeeding mothers' milk is a case in point. As Doug Murray summarizes with reference to Latin America:

> Pesticides contributed mightily to the increase in wealth and productivity in Central America, but so too did they contribute to the increase in misery in the region. Hidden within the ecological transformations that allowed cotton farming to thrive was an ecological crisis that played a significant role in the demise of the cotton

sector. Degraded land and water, escalating pest problems, resurgence of malaria and other diseases, all combined with high rates of pesticide poisoning do seriously affect the well-being of rural society in the cotton-growing region (1994: 54).

About 11 percent of global pesticide sales and 24 per cent of insecticides can be attributed to cotton production (Myers & Stolton, 1999). The World Bank cites price factors and lack of local knowledge or the misinformation of farmers as the main factors leading to excessive or inappropriate pesticide use (Farah, 1994). Doug Murray and Peter Taylor (2000), for example, show quite conclusively that campaigns for the safe use of pesticides (paid for and run by pesticide industries) are clearly constructed around the idea that persistent and high-level pesticide use are necessary and desirable, thus shaping the problem in a particular framework.

The processing of cotton into garments is also riddled with environmental problems. The cotton is treated with various chemicals to facilitate the processing stage and the bleaching and dyeing of the cloth or garment also leads to exposure to carcinogenic substances by both product and worker. The textile dyeing industry labor force is routinely exposed to carcinogenic substances (Michaelowa & Michaelowa, 1996: 52).

Another environmental problem associated with textile/cotton production is water pollution. Plantations may require higher rates of irrigation than water available in the region. Further down in the production chain, during the processing and dyeing stage, water will be discharged into rivers or streams and thus also affect drinking water. These problems will be discussed in more detail in relation to West Africa in chapter 6.

In many ways, the environmental problems associated with garments are worst at the individual household level as the production process is only about a relatively small part of the environmental burden. As Kate Fletcher and her colleagues argue in Dorothy Myers and Sue Stolton:

> The use stage [of textiles] has major environmental impacts. A lifecycle study by the American Fiber Manufacturers Association of a synthetic fiber blouse showed that as much as 88 per cent of atmospheric emissions, 86 per cent of energy and 68 per cent of solid waste attributable to the total textile lifecycle are massed during washing and drying. These results, however, should be placed in context. Only garments were studied and results could be significantly affected by a change in laundering habits. If the garment is washed at cold temperatures and dried on a line, total energy consumption is reduced by 78 per cent and the bulk of the environmental impacts would be in production rather than in use (Fletcher et al., 1999: 46).

This point again raises issues about the analytical distinction between production and consumption in the global political economy and the need for the inclusion of consumption as a field of study. It also shows that some activities cannot be regulated as they are social practices not open to regulation. For example, people's laundry habits cannot be subjected to legal patterns regardless of their environmental impact. They can only be influenced through waste water charges. There is a public-private distinction in this field.

In any case, the environmental regulation in the political economy of textiles cannot be focused in textiles or in cotton itself. Rather, it has to take place through agricultural regulation and through the regulation of certain chemicals involved in the process, etc.; the global cotton garment or textile chain in general has not been controlled or regulated at the international or global level. However, some national or regional regulations have an effect on the global textile chain. For example, Banuri reports that the German government has outlawed garments containing azo dyes (1998: III/5). This means that a flouting of this legislation may lead to shipments being burned at the manufacturer's expense. Other European states have followed suit with similar legislation. Since European consumers make up a significant share of global textile consumption, such regional legislation obviously has an impact on production patterns elsewhere. However, it has to be admitted that a substantial share of textile imports to Germany still contain azo dyes and that the laws are not strictly enforced. Although these measures have a limited success, the German ban on azo dyes still has implications for the nature of the textile trade and for the working of the international political economy because of the market clout of such a measure. Therefore, this strategy has at least some success and makes a case for 'unilateral action'.

There are no specific attempts to regulate the pesticide use in the garment sector at the international level. In the food sector, the Food and Agricultural Organization (FAO) and the World Health Organization (WHO) have established the Codex Alimentarius Commission that has commented on and recommended 'safe' pesticide levels since 1966. However, the Codex's primary goal is to harmonize legislation between different states rather than to introduce health and safety or environmental regulations. In addition, it deals only with food-related agricultural problems, not other agricultural fields. There are other problems relating to this organization that cannot be discussed here (Sklair, 2002: 144). A major problem with this organization and with other FAO and OECD working groups on pesticides is that the chemical industry is heavily represented in these working groups and has a strong influence in shaping pesticide control policy. This approach, therefore, provides a limited scope for the introduction of environmental concerns into an economic framework.

Pesticides are an issue in Agenda 21 of the Rio Conference. Agenda 21 is calling for the reduction of pesticide use and for integrated pest management. However, the term integrated pest management can be interpreted as ranging from conventional pest management to ecological farming methods. Although Agenda 21 does not specifically mention pesticides in textile production, it refers to agricultural, not only food, production in general.

Another approach to controlling the environmental consequences of the global textile trade has been through eco-labeling. This policy has been particularly popular on the European continent. It implies that a product undergoes certain tests stipulated by the national regulatory authority or by another named institution and if the product fulfills these conditions, it will be awarded the specific eco-label. The most well-known eco-label is the Blue Angel in Europe. Eco-labeling has been criticized because the criteria used for rewarding the label have been controversial. In the textile sector, eco-labeling products has been limited to awarding azo-dye free products with a label or products that do not contain certain named chemicals (but are not chemical-free). Therefore this approach is limited and has not had any real impact on the global textile chain as it is a voluntary code that has a limited value. Even supranational voluntary codes have been of limited effect unless their message gets taken up by consumers in a big way. This has not been the case with eco-labeled textiles which, in addition, are not widely available. Again, this is an unpromising approach.

An analysis of these existing forms of regulation or lack thereof suggests that in some areas of the textile chain a global regulatory 'regime' is not necessarily essential and would not effectively deal with any problems that would arise. The case of the azo dyes shows that regional regulatory efforts can have an impact on the global textile chain. However, in the case of pesticide pollution, such a scheme would not work. In this case a state-based regulatory approach does not seem very promising. Therefore different problems in the cotton garment chain require different solutions.

CONCLUSION

Global change in the textile industry and the manifestation of global change at the local level are characterized by the intended and unintended consequences of this production chain. Environmental degradation is largely an unintended consequence of changes in the global political economy. The degradation in working conditions and labor rights in the garment sector are direct responses to post-Fordist developments toward economies of flexibility. As such the consumer is alienated from the production process and not aware of the deteriorating health and safety and working conditions in textile processing. However, the nature of the distribution of purchasing power and concept of Western human rights and equality mean that consumer demand for cheaper clothing has to be countered with ethical and moral concerns that consumers need to be confronted with.

This chapter has tried to establish some connections between local socio-cultural practices in the North and production processes in developing countries. It has been argued that the global political economy has evolved in this direction; however, such terminology denies the existence of agency in this process. Attempts to deal with environmental degradation in the global textile economy need to take account of the social and structural origins of this degradation as well as the agents involved.

Chapter 6

The Case of West Africa

In this chapter, the subject matter of cotton and textiles will be looked at from the angle of a particular region, West Africa. West Africa has seen a recent drastic increase in cotton production in the past decade and is also seen as a region that has very much dropped out of the bottom of the global economy. The quantity of cotton lint production for the whole region of Western Africa increased from 510,873 tons in 1990 to 887,419 tons in 2001, the last year for which figures are available (FAOSTAT, 2002). However, at the same time the value of cotton lint exports decreased from $544,811,000 in 1990 to $487,781,000 in 2000 despite this huge increase. This chapter will show that West Africa is very much part of a globalizing political economy, if not in the same way as the Tiger states or the industrialized West.

First, a brief overview of the history of West Africa and its position in the international system over time will provide the necessary background introduction to understanding its position today. This overview will be followed by an analysis of the political economy of West Africa today. West Africa is here referred to as a coherent unit of analysis although this is obviously not necessarily the case. The subregions within West Africa can differ substantially from each other in varying issue areas; this will be pointed out when relevant.

No analysis of the political economy of developing countries can be complete without relating it to the debt crisis and global institutional policy. This will be the focus of the next section that investigates the impact of the debt crisis and the role of structural adjustment policies in this part of the world. Then a link will be made between structural adjustment and general economic policy and linking this to social and environmental degradation in the region. The aim here is not to establish some sort of causality between slave labor or environmental degradation and the demands/pressures of the global political economy but rather seeing what sort of mechanisms underlie all of these phenomena.

The second half of the chapter will be exclusively dedicated to the study of the global political textile economy in West Africa, particularly cotton.

Rather than focusing on the microlevel, the aim will be to outline and understand the linkages between globalizing trends and local phenomena. Thus there is a microlevel element in this analysis bringing together local and global linkages.

BACKGROUND

The African and by extension naturally the West African political economies are heavily influenced by their colonial experiences. The dependence on, and the influence of, cotton in the West African colonies was discussed in chapter 5, which showed the historical significance of cotton for the region, the power relations between colonized and colonizer, and the effects this has had on agricultural and thus on social patterns and life forms. In effect, even the slave trade that dominated Africa's external relations from about 1500 to 1800 was linked to cash crop agriculture. The trade in slaves delayed and also discouraged the use of African soil for cash crops as this would have a negative impact on the availability of slaves for trade, the future slaves being tied up in plantations in Africa (Wallerstein, 1986: 14). With decolonization the French and British political systems of representation were copied and used for African states. Thus it is possible to talk of African political economies while at the same time acknowledging that the economic and socio-cultural makeup of West African societies are fundamentally quite different. At first sight oil-rich Nigeria and resource-poor Mali do not seem to have all that much in common. Not all West African states are Francophone and the different colonial experiences influence life today. The common ground between Western African states is mostly found in issue areas that can be painted with a broad brush: colonial experience, agricultural economies, debt servicing, structural adjustment programs, multi-ethnic/tribal societies, and peripheral status in the world economy to name but a few.

Decolonization took place in the 1950s and 1960s and provided the basis for the post-colonial state. Chazan et al. summarize this situation:

> Although colonial governments retained many indigenous social institutions and brought about redefinition of others, colonial rule superimposed a new administrative structure on these social and political orders. This colonial apparatus of power operated within newly delineated boundaries. Even the French federal structures of French West Africa and French Equatorial Africa clearly distinguished between component territories (later to become the independent French-speaking states of Africa) on a geographic basis, thus superimposing physical definitions of frontiers on indigenous (and still

widely held) African perceptions of boundaries as belts of separation between social units (Chazan et al., 1999: 42).

The post-colonial world included administrative hierarchies based on the colonial civil service that was essentially a military-administrative unit (Chazan et al., 1999: 43). Thus, 'the formal agencies transferred to African hands were alien in derivation, functionally conceived, bureaucratically designed, authoritarian in nature and primarily concerned with issues of domination rather than legitimacy' (ibid.: 43). This had major consequences for domestic and foreign politics as Hoogvelt posits:

> Nation-statism was a colonial legacy with shallow roots in Africa's own history. In the absence of a home-grown capitalist bourgeoisie and strong civil society traditions, the bureaucratic state was fashioned and bankrolled to perform a welfare and accumulation role by an international policy consensus that cared more about land access than the promotion of democracy. As intermediaries between their peoples and financial resource flows from abroad, these states became the main source of income and the control of the state became a matter of survival. Whether one characterizes the African post-colonial state as weak, patrimonial, clientelist or merely inefficient and corrupt, the fact remains that these states imploded when the international community, led by the IMF [International Monetary Fund] and World Bank, called in their loans and rolled out a new agenda for Africa (1997: 317).

This shows the contradictory role of the state in contemporary Africa. On the one hand, there are very strong bureaucratic organizations that can be seen in the agricultural sector with its marketing boards, agricultural societies, and strong parastatal presence. On the other hand, all this is increasingly anachronistic in a liberalized and privatized global economy that frowns upon these constraints and controls. So, the African state cannot provide the type of governance expected by international economic governance but at the same time provides other forms of governance that are not really in harmony with global economic structures. This inherent contradiction makes itself known in the form of disorganization and lack of connection to global trends other than those imposed by the multilateral economic institutions. This is manifested, for example, in the lack of the development of a textile industry to complement the agricultural importance of cotton agriculture (Mshomba, 2000), the decoupling of the local cotton market from the global cotton market through the intermediary role of the cotton companies/marketing boards, and thus the precedence of bureaucratic structures over free market economics. While these structures have undeniable advantages for the population and farmers, they also give the civil service an inordinate amount of leverage over agricultural markets, which is often not supported by an understanding of, or interest in, the farming community. For countries largely dependent on agriculture for export earnings, such a situation can be potentially disastrous.

West African countries, with the exception of Ghana, can be found toward the bottom of the Human Development Index. They are largely primary commodity producers and are agricultural rather than industrial economies. About two hundred million people live in the region of ECOWAS, the regional economic integration organization for West Africa. The Francophone part of the region has a common currency, the CFA Franc (West African currency) that gives the region some form of common economic identity and a common market. One trend is the increasing formal economic integration of the different African regions. The perceived advantages of integration are the uneven spread of resources and facilitated access through integration, securing markets for domestic manufactured goods, increased bargaining position at the global level, and joint mobilization of resources. One may notice that these are all economic aims and that the social and cultural integration so prevalent in, for example, Europe is not a major aim. For example,

> The areas in which ECOWAS seeks to promote cooperation and development among member states are industry, transport, telecommunications and energy, agriculture, natural resources, commerce, monetary and financial matters as well as social and cultural affairs. The goal of all this is to raise the living standards of the people of the sub-region (Aryeetey & Oduro, 1996: 24).

There are many practical obstacles to this integration approach. For example, civil servants do not seem to be well-informed about the trade agreements in place and therefore cannot implement them. The agreements tend to be negotiated at the state level without the usual lobbying from non-state actors that can be found elsewhere. As Sam Asante comments:

> Another feature is the poor participation of the private sector in African economic organization. In fact, when it comes to integration in Africa we consider this a governmental affair. So the private sector is not involved in the drafting of the various protocols and their implementation.

> The lack of commitment of the ruling classes is another important problem. . . . African countries are generally very poor countries and when you ask for their commitment, you adopt a type of integration

approach which compels them to sacrifice the little that they have, before they can derive any benefit from it (1996: 52).

What Asante refers to here is the foregone income from customs duty, import taxes etc. These are much valued incomes in the era of structural adjustment programs that take away other sources of revenue for the state. On the other hand, markets rather than states are the foremost principles of social and economic organization in West Africa (Diawara, 1998: 116). Thus, there is a complicated relationship between states and markets quite unique to the region.

DEBT AND STRUCTURAL ADJUSTMENT

West Africa is not immune to the problems that most developing countries are plagued with in terms of being bound into the global economy through the vagaries of the debt crisis. As a consequence, it is now engaged in repayment programs and structural adjustment situations. Thus West Africa is as firmly a part of the global market and subject to privatization and liberalization strategies in other parts of the world. Given the strong presence of the state in West African economic organization, this obviously causes problems of compatibility of approaches. Some argue that the major incompatibility lies in the fact that structural adjustment programs effect change at the level of economic organization without touching the fundamental structures of the economy (Ndegwa, 1997: 318). For example, more than fifty developing countries depend on three or fewer commodities for more than half their export earnings (Financial Times, October 16, 2001). This applies especially to the cotton-growing regions of West Africa. Thus structural adjustment programs are essentially economic management approaches rather than structural approaches per se. They look at how the economic resources of a particular country can be used most efficiently to produce economic gain on the global market and thus create wealth and debt repayment capital for the country in question. In the case of most African countries, the structural adjustment remedy is the export of primary commodities. However, such a policy does not offer any opportunity for the primary commodity exporter to alter its structural position in the global economy.

For example, here is an excerpt from the IMF report on Burkina Faso:

Executive directors commended the authorities for their continued sound economic policies, and noted, in particular, the prudent management of the cotton sector in the face of low international prices, with the bumper cotton crop contributing to poverty reduction and a rebound in the rate of economic growth. Directors stressed that further efforts to liberalize the cotton sector, lower the cost of energy, promote good governance and judiciary reform, and develop human capital will be essential to maintain steady and rapid growth, strengthen the external position and achieve durable poverty reduction. It will be important that these efforts are supported by good coordination of donor assistance (IMF Public Information Notice No. 02/49, May 1, 2002).

Here, no acknowledgment is given that Burkina Faso's performance is actually dependent on external factors such as international cotton prices, which in turn are dependent on supply and demand. The answer to the price predicament is increased production which, in turn, if all cotton producers follow that path, will lead to hugely inflated supply and thus further drive prices down. Particularly ironic is the recommendation to further liberalize the cotton sector at a time where the international cotton price has halved over the period of several months due to oversupply on global markets. In addition, West African cotton has to compete with heavily subsidized cotton from the United States, which means that in effect there is no liberalized commodity market for cotton. Thus although Burkina Faso may improve its economic position by increasing cotton production (although this seems unlikely in the current situation), it cannot alter its structural position in the world economy. The IMF has recognized this dilemma in connection with other West African cotton producers but has made no qualitative statement regarding the situation:

> Directors considered that, given the cotton sector's crucial role in the economy, the reforms in this sector will be critical to Mali's medium-term economic prospects, as these constitute a key component of the structural reform. They therefore regretted the delay in undertaking key reforms in this sector, and urged the authorities to complete these reforms as quickly as possible in early 2002. In this regard, they were encouraged by the authorities' efforts to continue building consensus on the need to liberalize the cotton sector, especially since this would help ensure that the reform agenda is adopted by the post-election administration in 2002. Some directors noted that price supports and cotton subsidies in developed countries have tended to amplify the decline in cotton prices. The view also was held that other factors such as the decline in global demand and the demand for cotton specifically as a result of technological change have contributed to the difficulties in the sector (IMF Public Information Notice No. 02/2, January 9, 2002).

Brett argues that the failure of structural adjustment programs to lead to increased wealth for the inhabitants of developing countries is down to the fact that primary commodity producers (mostly farmers) are not paid a fair price for their merchandise (1997: 323). Thus the long arm of the state and the civil service (created by colonialism) are to blame for the lack of success of structural adjustment programs in bringing about increased wealth.

Brett's argument refers to the organization of the domestic economy while Stephen Ndegwa focuses on a developing country's position within the global economy. Both points go to the heart of the main problems associated with structural adjustment programs. The role of state bureaucracies in post-colonial West Africa clearly hinders the introduction of free markets and private enterprise. However, these state bureaucracies also prevent the evolution of fair prices for agricultural producers rather than looking after its population and ensuring a certain standard of welfare. Essentially, post-colonial bureaucracies take on the role of self-serving elites rather than social responsibilities.

This is one feature the post-colonial civil service has in common with the international economic institutions: the preservation of the status quo. Just as structural adjustment programs from a global perspective ensure the continued supply of primary commodities at cheap prices, they also make sure that primary commodity-producing states cannot really move away from the bottom of the food chain. Thus, structural adjustment policies do not deal with the structures of underdevelopment that the World Bank itself identifies as partly rooted in Africa's socio-economic and cultural history and partly rooted in Africa's position in the global economy (Ndegwa, 1997: 319). Structural adjustment may lead to more trade and go hand in hand with other trade liberalization moves but the classical critique of the free trade paradigm still holds: free trade and economic liberalization may lead to competitive advantages being fully used but at the end relative gains can make you absolutely worse off. The distinction between relative and absolute gains still applies and if one looks at overall world economic growth figures over several decades, then the gap between rich and poor has increased substantially while everybody is relatively better off than before.

Another very acute problem for West Africa is the extremely skewed nature of the world trade rules and regulations. Developing countries had high hopes for the liberalization of agriculture after the Uruguay Round but the existence of subsidies, and particularly export subsidies, means that West African agricultural products suffer both on the world market with low prices but also from subsidized imports that undercut local agriculture. Again, the root of the problem lies in West Africa's structural position in the world economy but also in the lack of understanding of the problems of farming communities in the local civil service.

All of the economic problems in West Africa cannot be blamed on structural adjustment programs. Indeed, many of the austerity programs are a reaction to public debt rather than to structural adjustment although the two

are obviously related. One of the biggest blows to the West African economies and one that led directly to the increase of cotton production is in the
foreign currency field rather than traditional structural adjustment. The 1994
devaluation of the CFA Franc (West African currency) had dramatic repercussions on the regional economy (Diawara, 1998: 104).

Although it is undoubtedly true that this reduction in price of West
African goods and services made them more competitive on the global market, it also decreased profit margins and income from the goods and services
offered. Thus a substantially higher amount needs to be sold in order to
achieve the same level of income as before.

Thus, new ways of creating foreign exchange and of recuperating the lost
profits needed to be found. This is where the dramatic increase in cotton
production since the mid-1990s fits in. Cotton is a primary commodity for
which there is high demand on global markets with its ever-increasing amount
of consumption—but also decreasing prices. Although domestic demand for
cotton has been increasing in West Africa as well and some of the increases
can be explained with this increased domestic demand, the majority of the
new cotton plantations' outputs are destined for export markets.

Another aspect of structural adjustment policies in Africa is the call for
state-building by the international economic institutions and the ensuing need
for efficient public institutions. However, Michael Kevane and Pierre Englebert
argue: "A country like Burkina Faso might not be in dire need of more state
capacity. Indeed, there is such a thing as too much capacity so that the state
drains the very best human resources away from wealth-creating activities
and into a status-laden administrative hierarchy" (1999: 262). In a comparative study of the West African and Sahelian region, Kevane and Englebert
conclude that there are significant differences between the various states of
the region and that general policies on state building valid for all states will
not be institutionally effective. However, dependence on agricultural exports
and among cotton production as one of the most important export commodities is a common defining element of the region and thus the region can be
defined as sharing economic problems but being diverse in political and socio-
cultural infrastructure. This has a partial effect on the cotton industry.

THE COTTON SECTOR

Most cotton production in West Africa, as in the rest of Africa, is regulated
through cotton marketing boards, called cotton companies in some states,
which are parastatal organizations taking over most of the commercial roles
relating to cotton production, such as purchase and distribution of seeds and
fertilizers as well as pesticides, direct purchasing of cotton from the farmer,

and determination of price (Sonapra in Benin, about to be privatized; Sofitex in Burkina Faso owned a third each by the state, the farmer's union, and the Compagnie Française pour le Développment des Textiles and the Compagnie Malienne pour le Développment des Textiles in Mali). Thus these boards play a major role in cotton production in West Africa although the IMF is increasing pressure to achieve more liberalization in the sector. The existence of these boards is said to be inefficient and to create high costs as well as low prices for producers (Gibbon, 1999: 129) but on the other hand, they are guaranteed markets for farmers and give stability from that perspective. So, although farmers are exposed to the price fluctuations of the global commodity markets, they are protected from the immediate supply and demand fluctuations that would affect their ability to sell.

As it is, the fluctuations are in production itself with its dependence on environmental factors for yield. For example, adverse weather conditions affected yields in Francophone Africa in 1998 and 1999 (www.clickforcotton .com/production.html). The following indicates the importance of cotton in the region:

Benin and Chad were the only two countries in Francophone Africa which increased cotton production in 1999/2000. Production in Benin rose by 8,000 tons to 150,000 tons in 1999/2000 while cotton output in Chad increased by 19 per cent to 76,000 tons. Chad's economy is dominated by the agricultural sector. Cotton, the major cash crop, accounted for 59 per cent of Chad's exports in 1998. Due to record cotton production in 1997/98, Chad's real gross domestic product increased by 8.1 per cent in 1998. In 1998/99, a decline in the return of the cotton sector led to a 1.1 per cent decline in real GDP in 1999. Despite the increase in cotton output in 1999/2000, the revenue from the cotton sector is not expected to recover substantially due to low international prices.

Cotton production in Mali declined by 12 per cent to 190,000 tons in 1999/2000, while rainy weather deteriorated cotton quality. Cotton is Mali's main cash crop, accounting for about 10 per cent of its GDP and 50 per cent of its total export receipts. Mali is the leading producer and exporter of cotton in Sub-Saharan Africa. Cotton is produced in an area inhabited by about 2.5 million people with 96 per cent of the population engaged in production. Given the importance of the cotton sector in Mali, it is expected that the dramatic decline in cotton production during 1999/2000 will have a significant impact on the overall economy (www.clickforcotton.com/production.html).

Cotton Lint Export Figures

Cotton lint exports Qty (mt)	1990	1993	1994	1995	1996	1997	1998	1999	2000
Western Africa	327,661	428,784	380,873	427,943	433,087	500,237	577,684	497,412	552,411
Benin	41,079	60,000	74,000	98,804	89,000	112,000	107,000	84,000	100,100
Burkina Faso	58,664	60,000	40,000	55,304	42,000	60,500	96,000	69,000	73,600
Côte d'Ivoire	89,340	95,561	100,282	88,283	74,531	85,500	116,500	122,000	160,652
Gambia	1,347	1,300	1,100	623	642	260	320	200	200
Ghana	N/A	1,800	7,200	500	0	1	1,119	6,520	10,397
Guinea	1,622	9,836	5,540	6,600	4,748	3,900	5,000	9,000	4,450
Guinea-Bissau	263	630	500	670	1,200	800	800	1,100	1,000
Mali	92,656	133,176	90,000	105,000	130,000	140,000	160,000	138,000	164,100
Niger	1,490	900	900	350	2,200	2,600	1,072	1,072	1,503
Nigeria	2,784	3,450	2,900	2,006	22,000	32,000	8,900	8,900	190
Senegal	5,066	19,789	15,242	9,079	10,893	14,576	14,473	4,620	6,698
Togo	33,260	42,342	43,209	60,724	55,873	48,100	66,500	53,000	29,521

Source: FAOSTAT, 2002.

These figures illustrate the importance of cotton production for countries like Mali and other West African countries while at the same time showing how much these agricultural sectors are bound into the global economy. The declining world cotton price (responding to supply but also to fashion) as well as the weather can decide on the economic performance of a whole region or country. For example, in 2001 economic growth slowed substantially in Mali as a result of the crisis in the cotton sector and lower rainfall (IMF News Brief No 02/78, July 26, 2002). In Benin the sharp decrease in world cotton prices had limited effect in 2001 because most exports had been realized in the first half of the year before the cotton prices depressed (IMF Public Information Notice No. 02/79, August 5, 2002).

It is pertinent here to compare the relative cotton dependence of the various West African states. Rather than just using production figures, export figures are also used as they indicate the role of cotton in a country's external relations rather than home use.

These figures show that those countries that rely heavily on cotton production increased their export production as a result of the 1994 currency devaluation. On the other hand, not all countries put their eggs in one basket. This is dependent on the geographical conditions and choices open to the countries as well as recommendations by agricultural marketing boards and international organizations.

Overall, Western Africa increased its cotton production by roughly 750,000 tons between 1990 and 2000. Benin, Burkina Faso, Guinea, Mali, and Togo

Cotton Lint Production Figures

Cotton lint production Qty (mt)	1990	1994	1998	2000	2001
Western Africa	510,873	584,037	898,065	807,421	887,419
Benin	59,210	103,209	150,069	152,000	141,000
Burkina Faso	77,318	66,594	136,314	109,000	114,000
Côte d'Ivoire	107,494	115,591	114,059	177,150	124,500
Gambia	654	1,200	220	230	230
Ghana	5,015	9,340	18,300	19,000	20,000
Guinea	2,070	6,607	15,844	29,600	29,600
Guinea-Bissau	1,000	600	900	1,200	1,200
Mali	114,645	128,096	219,216	100,800	230,000
Niger	920	3,200	1,400	6,442	6,889
Nigeria	95,000	80,000	135,000	145,000	145,000
Senegal	14,000	18,800	4,811	8,899	15,000
Togo	33,547	50,800	69,104	58,100	60,000

Source: FAOSTAT, 2002.

substantially increased their production and in some cases more than doubled it. On the other hand, countries such as Gambia, Ghana, Nigeria, and Senegal only marginally increased their production or even decreased it. However, all of the major cotton producers substantially increased production.

In terms of exports, overall Western Africa increased its exports by about 217,000 tons between 1990 and 2000. However, the value of cotton lint exports decreased from \$544,811,000 in 1990 to \$487,781,000 in 2000 as a result of the decline in cotton prices (FAOSTAT, 2002). The value of exports decreased quite dramatically between 1998 and 1999 although production was more or less the same. However, less cotton was exported, which can be attributed to a fall in prices on world cotton markets. The West African Common Market and the CFA common currency zone also account for cross-border traffic and some figure distortion.

The conclusions that can be drawn from these data are that cotton has taken over an increasingly large part of many of the Western African states' agricultures and this has obviously had repercussions on all sorts of other areas of the social and economic sphere. First, cotton producers are not only dependent on world commodity prices but also on such a whimsical concept as fashion. Western fashions move from cotton to synthetic fibers and back again and these have repercussions on prices and demand. The past few years have seen the comeback of synthetic fibers as well as linen for many garments while cotton was extremely fashionable in the early 1990s, thus fueling demand for the 1990s.

Second, as larger areas of agricultural land are given over to cotton, this decreases crop diversity, crop rotation, and spreading of risk. Such a policy increases vulnerability to world market prices but also to pest attacks, adverse weather conditions, and crop diversity. The environmental consequences will be discussed in a separate section.

Third, there are questions of human and food security. Again, the problems relating to environmental issues and human security will be discussed in the next section. As in colonial times, increased land use for cotton can take land away that was originally reserved for food production, thus necessitating the import of foodstuffs. However, Tobias Reichert seems to suggest that this is not such a serious problem as it is perceived to be with the possible exception of Benin (2000: 6).

THE TEXTILES AND GARMENT SECTOR

Unlike South East Asia and Latin America, the textiles and garment sectors are not very well developed in Western Africa and are also not geared for export production. Most production is for local consumption. Therefore the discussion on the social conditions of garment production discussed in chapter 5 does not apply to West Africa. The development of a textiles industry is generally seen as a higher stage of development and one that Western Africa, or most of Africa in general, has not reached yet. The IMF has recommended, for example, that the Mali government undertakes steps to diversify its economic base by developing a textile industry (Public Information Notice No. 02/2, January 9, 2002).

The phasing out of the Multi Fiber Arrangement and the subsuming of the textiles trade under World Trade Organization (WTO) rules need not necessarily have strong consequences for the region. As most textile production is not geared for export, it remains unaffected by these rules. In addition, West African states enjoy preferential treatment through the Lomé convention with the European Union. Given the cheap labor and the availability of local cotton in West Africa, it would lend itself as a primary location for an export textile industry. However,

> These two factors alone are not sufficient to develop a viable and competitive textiles and apparel industry. To develop such an industry also takes political and macroeconomic stabilities, good infrastructure, skilled labor and management, and policies that encourage and protect investment. These have been identified to be the key elements that have contributed to the Mauritian success (Mshomba, 2000: 131).

Most of the production for local use takes place in the informal sector for which there are no data. However, the existing if unreliable data sets seem to suggest that Ghana and Nigeria have the larger (formal) textile sectors compared with the other states in the region (Reichert, 2000: B4). These are two states without a well-developed cotton-growing industry.

Another issue suppressing the development of local or export-oriented textile and garment industries is the existence of second-hand clothing markets that are the main source of garment supply. The rural population is in large part dependent on cheap second-hand clothing imports for their garment needs.

There are effectively two types of garments on sale for the general public in Africa, the indigenous type of clothing and the second-hand clothing from mostly the United States and Western Europe. The indigenous clothing industries for everyday wear is mostly not able to compete with imports or second-hand clothing on grounds of quality, style, or price.

Karen Hansen, an anthropologist, reports that second-hand clothing, which used to be for the very poor and frowned upon in the past, has become extremely popular for all segments of society as a source of style, fashion, and individuality (1999). It is an affordable form of clothing and also appeals to popular taste. There is no shame involved in wearing these clothes and constructions about North-South divide, cultural imperialism, etc. are subjects that are not discussed in Africa (1999: 345). Furthermore,

> The recent rapid growth of the international second-hand clothing trade is a product of ongoing unequal economic integration on a global scale. Yet the directions of the commodity flows that comprise this trade cut across conventional North-South and urban-rural divides, giving rise to new distinctions. Although the trade in second-hand clothing has a long history, its economic power and global scope were never as vast as they have been since the early 1990s in the wake of the liberalisation of many Third World economies and following the sudden rise in demand from former Eastern bloc countries. Worldwide second-hand clothing exports increased sixfold between 1980 and 1995. Sub-Saharan African countries are among the world's largest importers, with consumption of second-hand clothing exceeding that of all other regions (Hansen, 1999: 347).

It seems that everybody is content with this production-consumption cycle. The recipients of the second-hand clothes are happy because it gives them access to affordable Western-style clothes while the individual donors are happy that they can refill their wardrobes at regular intervals without feeling guilty about the waste or excessive consumption as their clothes will serve a charitable cause. Therefore concerns about the ethical nature of this trade seems to be a concern mostly of globalization critics and environmentalists.

Nevertheless, regardless of one's ideological persuasion, it remains a fact that it has become socially acceptable that one part of the world does the consuming and that the poorer, or less powerful, part of the world then gets the 'leftovers.' As the demands of the poor are lower, they are happy with the leftovers. This setup is indicative of serious equity problems and although everybody is happy in a pragmatic sense in the face of reality, this does not imply that everybody is equally happy about the structural inequality perpetuated by second-hand clothing markets, especially as they stifle indigenous industries. This point makes it very clear again that the issue and concept of consumption is very much at the forefront of contemporary practical and theoretical international political economy (IPE) and thus is part of a holistic approach.

THE ENVIRONMENTAL DIMENSION

The environmental dimension of cotton production in West Africa is woefully underresearched as are most cotton production areas. However, there are certain general environmental problems with cotton production and these can also be found in West Africa. The main problems are as follows.

Water supply and irrigation are particular problems in areas that are not naturally suited for cotton production and do not have the rainfall patterns or irrigation systems that are desirable for high-quality cotton production. Globally, about two thirds of all cotton is produced with irrigation systems and the yield of such methods is much higher than the rainfall-dependent crops. Irrigated cotton is mainly grown in arid climates where freshwater is not always easily available. Therefore, irrigation has a strong impact on the local water situation and especially on the supply of, and availability and state of, local or regional freshwater resources. Freshwater may be diverted away from other irrigation projects for cotton crops, thus affecting local food security. Likewise, demand for water may constrain cotton production.

There are several water-related pollution problems. For example, water withdrawal for extensive irrigation often leads to falling water tables and thus to the depletion of a valuable resource. In addition, taking water out of rivers can lead to supply shortages further along the river run. Ecosystems alongside the river area will alter with changing water tables and this will affect soil quality, water availability, local climate, as well as biodiversity. Likewise, extensive irrigation in dry climates can result in a direct salinization of soil (Soth, 1999: 6). Cotton is in the list of the top three most irrigation-intensive crops together with rice and wheat. As cotton needs an arid and hot climate for growth as well as a high level of irrigation, these conditions are rarely fulfilled without extensive manipulation of local water supplies. For example, in Mali water is taken out of the river Niger for cotton irrigation purposes as such intensive agriculture would not be possible otherwise. However, in general the vast majority of West African cotton is grown as a purely rain-fed crop. For example, there are no irrigated cotton plantations in Burkina Faso. Although this clearly limits the effects of irrigation-related environmental degradation, it makes the farms more dependent on weather conditions for a high yield and good quality crop.

In general, there are relatively simple solutions for the reduction of water usage in agricultural irrigation. As a WWF report states:

> From a technical perspective, new irrigation methods like drip irrigation or deficit irrigation promise a simple solution to increase water efficiency. However, the implementation of such technology runs into several obstacles. Firstly, drip or sprinkler irrigation systems need investment, energy and technical know-how in order to maintain and run, whereas flood irrigation needs only manual labour. Secondly, in countries with a long history of irrigation, traditional

flood or furrow irrigation systems are an integral part of their cultural
system of values, habits and traditions (Soth, 1999: 12).

Thus there are relatively simple solutions for managing the environmental
impact of irrigation projects by reducing the amount of water used. This
addresses part of the problem but does not go to the root of the problem that
is the use of soil for an agricultural crop that is not really suited for that type
of soil.

Another problem is that of agricultural chemicals. Related to this point,
agricultural runoff in the form of pesticides, fertilizers, and other chemicals
contaminate rivers, lakes, wetlands, and other freshwater resources. Thus,
these pollutants can influence or destroy biodiversity and ecosystem health
either through direct toxic impact or through accumulation in the system. As
it is, the unsuitability of most cotton growing areas for this crop means that
cotton crops are particularly vulnerable to pests and in need of more pesticides and fertilizers, thus creating a much higher demand for these substances. In fact, in the smallholder farms of Burkina Faso, for example, maize
and cotton are the only crops on which pesticides are used.

The problems with agrochemicals are manifold reaching from the acute
to long-term loss of soil fertility as well as to water pollution. In addition,
prolonged use of pesticides eventually leads to pest resistance that also has
implications for food-based agriculture. However, the most widely cited problem of pesticides are seen as health-related:

> Information gathering in cotton-producing countries as diverse as
> Egypt, Senegal, Sudan, India, Nicaragua and the USA by Pesticides
> Action Network (PAN) indicates that acutely toxic organophosphates
> are much in use on the cotton crop and that their use has been
> reported to cause health and environmental risks. Problems easily
> arise in conditions where people are illiterate or unaware of dangers,
> where proper equipment is unavailable or too expensive, clean water
> is absent or in short supply and where medical help is remote and
> costly. Figures for poisoning and deaths related to pesticide use reflect
> these problems. In developing countries, up to 14 per cent of all
> occupational injuries in the agricultural sector and 10 per cent of all
> fatal injuries can be attributed to pesticides (Myers and Stolton,
> 1999: 13).

Other figures suggest that most pesticide poisoning is actually caused by
inappropriate use of pesticides and likewise that pesticide runoff is also caused
by inappropriate and excessive use of pesticides. For example, during the
1999–2000 season at least thirty-seven people died of pesticide poisoning in

Benin (Pesticides News, March 2000: 74). As cotton pesticides are virtually the only pesticides available in the cotton-growing regions of Benin and the only ones delivered on a credit loan basis, they are also used on food crops, with often devastating and sometimes lethal consequences. The UNPCB (national union of cotton producers in Burkina Faso) also acknowledges that accidents with pesticides happen due to inexpert use but finds that more risks are involved with the use of herbicides but their use is not as widespread. Thus in the West African case, one can see a role for the parastatal cotton boards and farmers unions in this situation. As the suppliers of cotton seeds, fertilizers, pesticides, etc. they can and often do play an educational role in alerting to the dangers of the substances provided and their appropriate use. Given that the neoliberal principles of unfettered market forces do not apply in the domestic management of the agricultural sector in West Africa, there is actually room for training and also for economical use of these substances. Financial constraints already mean that farmers are economical in their use of pesticides. Poverty prevents farmers (and the environment) from excessive pesticide exposure. Thus West Africa is actually in a potentially (but not actually) better position than many of the farmers in, for example, India who are fully co-opted into the agrochemical circuit. It can safely be argued that West Africa is one region where the power of the agrochemical sector over local actors is still relatively minor. On the other hand, Doug Murray and Peter Taylor warn of the dangers of leaving training to parastatal organizations as this leaves pesticide producers 'off the hook' and puts the onus and responsibility for safe use solely and squarely on the farmers (2000).

Thus, the situation of the West African cotton industry cannot be easily compared with other cotton-producing regions because of the predominance of the smallholder farmer model. Cotton is the cash crop of choice because of the colonial experience and has historical significance rather than other rational criteria of selection. So far, environmental problems in the cotton farmer sector are the typical problems of intensive agriculture rather than specific problems unique to cotton. These problems exist with other cash crops as well. Farmers can minimize environmental effects by using three- or four-year cycles in their crop rotation patterns rather than two-year cycles practiced by many farmers at the moment. However, given that cotton is the only real export earner (or perceived by such by the civil service and multilateral agencies), it fetches the best price for the farmers and thus long cycles of crop rotation will substantially decrease the amount of cotton grown with all that entails. Thus there is a need for more crop diversity but this is not a farming or environmental policy issue but rather a domestic agricultural/ economic policy issue as well as a policy issue for the multilateral institutions that will be decided without environmental concerns at heart.

Finally, other environmental problems exist in the cotton-processing industries such as dying, tanning, or weaving. Again, this can result in water or
chemical pollution as well as in environmental pollution and health issues for
workers in the industries. These are problems more difficult to rectify than the
agricultural problems for the simple reason that there are no easy alternatives.
However, here it may seem an advantage that the West African textile industry is relatively undeveloped and exists primarily in the ethnic sector. Nevertheless, colorful dyes found in ethnic wear can be extremely toxic. Some less
toxic and more benign alternatives exist but these are not in wide use.

In comparing the environmental situation in West Africa over time, it can
be said that increasing technological sophistication has led to some changes
in the local nature-society relations that makes the current situation different
from the cotton-growing periods under colonialism. First of all, despite the
historically determined continuing important of cotton, ownership patterns
have changed although the actual ownership of land and other resources does
not seem to be the overriding factor. The civil service or parastatal organizations still have an important input into the agricultural decision-making process and this aspect has not changed fundamentally. However, neoliberal
market rules and the involvement of non-governmental organizations in the
agricultural process are slowly changing the form of cotton agriculture and
thus the privatization of nature is also at work in West Africa. There is a
general consensus among farmers that in this generation land degradation has
changed to such an extent that it is unprecedented and gives concern for
future generations. This is due to the largely increased demand on the land.

The nature of the environmental problems in cotton agriculture in West
Africa make the time dimension relatively simple and one of mostly crop
rotation cycles having to fit soil regeneration cycles. However, a more press-
ing time dimension is that of the compatibility of social time in the West
African region and in the developed world. Both the ecological and social
conditions in West Africa and West Africa's linkages with other regions show
that the need for cash crop generation has led to disembedded social and
cultural institutions as well as the need to intensive agriculture. This impact
on environment-society relations is particularly driven by the influence of
global governance constraints.

This becomes nowhere clearer as in the world trade field: Another principle of the neoliberal world economy has a huge structural impact on agriculture and that is international trade rules on agriculture. The Burkinabé
minister of agriculture notes that local farming produce is undercut on the
local markets by imports subsidized by their states of origin, thus pushing
farmers even more toward cash crops (Interview, Sedelan). However, in the
second half of 2001 the global cotton price has hit rock bottom as a direct
result of oversupply due to farming subsidies paid to farmers in the United

States and Europe. Thus the combination of free market with no import levies and subsidies in other parts of the world are having disastrous social as well as environmental consequences in West Africa. These problems can only be overcome through fairer, regulated prices, most obviously through taxation of incoming agricultural produce. However, this is not an option under the current world trade framework. When the Mali and Benin governments extended financial help to their cotton sectors in 2001, this was frowned upon by the International Monetary Fund (IMF) that illustrates the equity problems of current global structures in the clearest possible way.

The main difference over the past one hundred years or so is that of a shift from overt power to structural power. Under colonialism, direct coercion was used or threatened in order to achieve cotton production over other types of production. Today, nobody forces West African states to grow cotton; however, the global political economy and structural adjustment make it necessary to produce cash crops for export and cotton is a good export earner for these states. In a state with no industry, going beyond subsistence agriculture to cash crop production is the only way to generate economic surplus for much-needed imports and the existing international economic structures do not consider the needs of the rural population and their environment in West Africa.

The technological impact of modern fertilizers and pesticides has led to environmental impacts that did not exist in this form in the 1880s. This is not to say that no environmental degradation existed in conjunction with cotton farming in colonial times; rather that the agrochemical economy has added a global dimension from a structural perspective. To return to the argument about modes of production and capitalism as the structural origin of environmental degradation discussed in chapters 1–4, it can be argued here that local environmental degradation certainly existed in the 1880s caused by international economic pressures. However, the environmental degradation in the cotton sector in West Africa today has wider-reaching environmental impacts than its colonial predecessor. What has changed, is the extent of the spread of this form of environmental degradation and this is an issue related to technological progress and population pressures rather than to different forms of capitalism. This argument again supports a view of ecological world systems theory rather than the traditional Marxist and modernist view of modern capitalism triggering environmental degradation per se. Although cotton was not grown for export in pre-capitalist societies and therefore no comparison can be made, it remains clear that the structural conditions of cotton production are essentially the same under colonialism and today. The same cannot be said about cotton consumption, however. Thus the fundamental changes in the global cotton economy can be found at a non-local level although its impact is clearly tangible at the local level. Again, an eco-holistic approach can lead to understanding the complexities of this interplay. Thus the basic tenets of the ecological world systems perspective are confirmed in the West African case: both the economic and environmental problems of the region mirror its position in the global political economy and are intrinsically linked. It is an ideal illustration of the equity, consumption, trade, time, and governance issues raised in Section I. Although its marginalization in the globalization process also means that the severity of the privatization of nature problems is not as acute as elsewhere on the planet, the lack of integration at a higher structural level in the international system perpetuates and aggravates West Africa's position in the world, leaving little room for ecological, social, and welfare improvement.

Chapter 7

Conclusion

This book has looked at the various perspectives relating to environment and society and the global political economy and has advocated shifting the focus of mainstream analysis to include a new concept of environment-society relations based on a different historical interpretation of the origins of environmental degradation. At the same time, an eco-holistic political economy approach, as indeed any critical political economy approach, needs to include an understanding of the institutions of consumption and equity in order to offer holistic analysis.

The increasing gulf between North and South, which cannot only be analyzed through the typical class or other inequality channels, is the most visible manifestation of the relevance of a consumption and equity focused analysis. As a general rule, the messier, unreliable, and basic aspects of production are located in the South while consumption of goods takes place in the North (this statement ignores resource extraction as an industry for which other rules apply). Thus, this new North-South divide leads to an ever-increasing inequality that goes far beyond the structural imbalances found, for example, under colonialism. It is also supported by an international institutional framework that is geared toward keeping the status quo in this production-consumption dichotomy despite paying lip service to the abolition of these inequalities.

STRUCTURAL CONSTRAINTS IN PRACTICE

This section is concerned with the way in which policy can be used to affect the problem areas discussed in this book. It will first outline the parameters of the liberal institutionalism that underlies the existing policy framework and identify possible areas for change. This section will identify the arena within which managerial approaches are located and management solutions are offered and extend from that basis.

Starting with the issue of consumption, this approach does not form the basis of any existing institutional framework. However, the organization of production is very much institutionalized and within this framework consumption is seen as a natural extension of the production framework. This production framework has several dimensions that are comprised of a global division of labor, a trade liberalization movement, a global financial framework facilitating the free movement of capital as well as a lack of social, welfare, and environmental regulations built into the economic framework. These regulations are usually organized along separate lines and the World Trade Organization (WTO) framework has now made it clear that these regulations will have to be subordinated to the global trade framework even if prior international law on the subject existed. There is even an institutional framework for intellectual property rights that organizes the production and use of knowledge at the global level (Thomas, 2000: 72).

All these aspects of the global production, or economic, framework are set up on the basis of liberal economic thought as well as neoliberal market efficiency ideas. From this perspective, consumption is just a supply and demand variable. Likewise, environmental and social considerations are marginalized because they cannot be included in the particular type of rationality underlying the production framework.

This type of market efficiency that is focused on production and price mechanism and sees solutions as a pricing and efficiency issue, cannot take on board issues of consumption equity and distribution of wealth. It is based on accumulation of wealth ideas and cannot incorporate into its analytical framework the notion of structural inequality. As the structure of the economic or production framework in itself forbids the transfer of structural advantage and argues that entrepreneurship can lead to wealth accumulation, the structural basis of the distribution of resources is not addressed. With consumption being an equity policy issue, this problem could not be denied, however. The same applies to the other issue areas treated here.

The second issue is focused on nature-society or environment-society relations. Environment-society relations take place at various levels and thus are part of various institutional frameworks. However, in general they are organized along separate lines from other forms of social organization. The most obvious form of environmental policy framework can be found in the negotiation and putting into place of multilateral or international environmental agreements. These are on various issues, usually organized around a single-issue basis. So there are agreements on global warming, acid rain, marine pollution, or ozone depletion to name but a very few but these are not connected (or only peripherally) to the issues giving rise to the pollution in the first place. Again, there is a feasibility-necessity dichotomy as these agreements are based on politically and economically feasible solutions to environmental degradation rather than on environmentally necessary options.

The implications of this have been discussed in detail elsewhere (Kütting, 2000) and suffice it to say that a separation of environmental policy from other social and economic policy leads to the marginalization of environmental matters. This is also apparent in other fields besides international environmental agreements. Voluntary codes of conduct, for example, suffer from a similar predicament. Rather than being forced into formalized norms or commitments, economic actors prefer to subscribe to voluntary codes of behavior that they can set and implement themselves without control (Sajhau, 1997). From this point of view private and public forms of environmental regulation do not differ all that much.

Many international institutions have an environmental component or an environmental mission statement. In the international economic framework, the World Bank and the WTO have an environmental agenda while the International Monetary Fund (IMF) clearly has not. The World Bank's environmental policy is primarily related to the environmental impact of its lending and policy suggestions. After having been accused of environmental mismanagement, the Bank has become more environmentally conscious but this still happens within a traditional framework. The WTO's environmental agenda is still unclear and undeveloped although it is generally agreed that free trade and sustainable development should go hand in hand. In fact, free trade should lead to more sustainable development as it facilitates technology transfer of cleaner technologies. This is undoubtedly true but again neglects the understanding of the distribution of wealth and capital on the planet as well as seeing cleaner technology as an environmental management solution to deeper structural problems. Thus the discourse of sustainable development is in itself a policy option that neglects an understanding of environment-society relations but pays lip service to environmental protection. It also affects the last issue, that of equity problems, as a comprehensive sustainable development agenda does include issues of poverty and social justice.

The sustainable development discourse is strong on rhetoric for equal opportunities and for catching up but the practical terms are not clearly related to these goals. So, in terms of equity issues, these are addressed through the liberal and neoliberal framework of equality of opportunity and free market access and entrepreneurship leading to success. At the same time these developments should take place within the realms of clean production and technology in order to fulfill environmental demands. This will lead to the extension of cleaner economic sectors and to the gradual dying out of the dirtier ones. Thus we face a vision of a brave new world where everybody is wealthy in a clean environment. The obvious physical limitations to this vision are ignored. In addition, no international institution has changed its fundamental direction because of sustainable development.

The same applies to the issue of equity in the global system. Although there is lip service to the idea of fairness and to no exploitation, this is not actually present in any legal framework. Concerns about slavery or indecent working conditions are swept aside as moves to block such practices are seen as not practicable. For example, recent concerns about the use of slaves on West African cocoa plantations have led to public outcries and to demands that multinational corporations owning or buying from plantations are supposed to clean up their act and use their clout and influence to stop these practices. In turn, the multinationals involved have argued that it would be too expensive and non-feasible to ascertain if slavery is used in production processes; however, they are willing to spend millions for public relations campaigns protesting their repugnance of slavery. The same applies for the textile industry in South East Asia and for the headline-grabbing cases of Nike and the Gap. These companies spend millions developing codes of conduct and advertising this fact but less on actually implementing these codes. They conduct inspections of factories but these are done in collaboration with the factory rather than as a 'checkup.'

These issues raise questions about the private and public nature of regulating these issues. Private institutions such as codes of conduct and public-private initiatives between companies and members of civil society are often cited as the way forward to a clearing up of equity problems. Whole non-governmental organization (NGO) industries have developed on this premise. However, this raises questions about putting the wolf in charge of the sheep. Clearly, these private initiatives have only evolved as a response to public pressure and as a way to avoid public regulation. It is better to do something before one is made to do it. In turn, this self-regulation plays into the hands of the free market ideology as it emphasizes trade liberalization and self-regulation. It complements ideally the prevailing canon of economic ideology.

Thus, when regarding the policy option available within the prevailing institutional framework, it becomes obvious that structural changes will have to address the distribution of wealth and responsibility. However, such issues tend to be discredited as anachronistic and Marxist and are thus not very likely to become causes of the neoliberal institutional framework. The remainder of this chapter will examine avenues to overcome this feasibility-necessity dichotomy. There are essentially two ways these problems can be tackled. One of them is to have an effect on different localities through global means. The other is to influence the global through local means.

GLOBAL GOVERNANCE I:
REGULATING THE LOCAL THROUGH THE GLOBAL

Regulating the local through the global happens within global institutional frameworks. The advantage of this approach is the creation of global norms that will influence and form behavior at the local level. Thus it is all-pervasive and equally applicable to all parts of the world.

Examples of global norms influencing the local are institutional frameworks such as those of the United Nations, the World Trade Organization, the liberal framework of the Bretton Woods institutions in general, as well as socio-cultural phenomena. Other global norms established through private institutions are global business practices as well as investment practices. There is no need to explain these in much detail as they are well documented elsewhere except for socio-cultural phenomena. By these I mean consumer preferences such as fashions but also certain values relating to the desirability of behavior and consumption. So, for example, the proliferation of non-indigenous foodstuffs is a global socio-cultural phenomenon, albeit with different impact in different parts of the world. Likewise, tastes for sports such as soccer/football have become global norms that have repercussions on the perception of the nature and desirability of celebrity. These are global norms that can become informally socially institutionalized but are not part of a formal global framework and rather a side-product.

Environmental norms can be private or public. The most common form of environmental norms are international or multilateral environmental agreements the most well-known of which are the Montreal Protocol on the depletion of the ozone layer and the Kyoto Protocol on climate change. Private environmental norms are voluntary codes of practices of certain industrial sectors or by certain companies. These are more often found in the social rather than environmental field although informal arrangements between industry and governments exist in the environmental field as well.

Global environmental norms can have several effects. On the one hand, they can lead to a harmonization of norms and to an awareness creation in some parts of the world where the specific environmental problem had not received particular attention before. On the other hand, they can impose certain solutions to environmental problems that may not necessarily be in the best interest of all the participants in the regime. Thus there are benefits and drawbacks to these norms. The two main drawbacks are, first, that a global and harmonized solution to environmental problems does not take account of the various structural positions of the actors involved in the international system and thus is too rigid an approach. The concept of 'common but differentiated responsibility' is supposed to deal with the substance of this problem. However, it does so in an environmental management approach that is directed at doing away with the disagreements at the negotiation rather than at the structural level. Thus it is feasibility based rather than necessity based.

The second drawback is the disregard for the different positions of the different actors in an environmental problem. Populous and less populous, industrialized and agricultural states as well as different geographical as well as structural positions cannot be built into global norms except through concepts such as the aforementioned common but differentiated responsibility, critical loads, or suchlike. This means that either global norms are extremely vague and only centered on principle or that they are not suitable for all states. Thus global environmental norms by definition have to be vague and cannot deal with specific problems of global structural constraints manifested at the local level.

Although global environmental problems necessitate global solutions, global solutions by themselves cannot solve a global environmental problem. In addition, global environmental problems manifest themselves in different ways in different regions of the world and although global awareness surely helps the solution of this problem, it cannot be the only approach given the various local situations.

Social norms in the context of this book, i.e. relating to equity considerations, are usually in the private domain. Of course there are various UN conventions on, for example, human rights or child labor but these are mostly statements of principle rather than concrete policy tools. Particularly in the textile industry, norms are usually institutionalized through voluntary codes of conduct. Although these have their advantages in that they are industry-specific and can thus deal with the problem in a direct and targeted manner, this is also their weakness as the guardians of the codes are also the perpetrators in the first place. Furthermore, these are company-specific codes rather than industry-wide regulations. However, potential advantages of such codes of conduct are that as industry-specific codes they work against the downward spiral of cheap labor in developing countries as they offer regulations across the industry in which developing countries cannot out-compete one another with cheaper labor and worse working conditions. As they stand, nevertheless, being company-specific codes with no enforcement agency but the company itself, the norms are not really sufficient and practice shows that they are not rigorously enforced.

However, the practice of industry-specific regulation at the global level has much to commend it from both environmental and equity perspectives. Such regulation and its enforcement should be industry-specific but organized by an international outside body for independent inspection and implementation. In this way global norms could be specific enough to avoid the problems of many other global institutional practices.

Other approaches such as incorporating social and environmental issues under the WTO treaty are not very likely to succeed because they assume a level playing field and also a consensus in wanting these rights. As many developing countries see the downward spiral as a competitive advantage, such policies are unlikely to be part of the WTO. In addition, it would be against the spirit of the WTO framework that is after all about the facilitation of trade rather than about the introduction of environmental protection and social equity—although environmental and social safeguards could surely be incorporated to a much larger and more effective extent.

Other global norms are formulated through the International Labor Organisation, for example. This UN organization has formulated many agreements on labor conditions and many of these have become global norms over time. However, most welfare and social frameworks such as these are usually subordinated to the rules of the market or to the neoliberal framework and are thus in a weak position in the international system. One option would be to elevate these agreements to equal status with the economic institutional framework and to enshrine this equality in international law. From this perspective, global social and environmental norms could be elevated in status. This would be of limited success however as their changed status would also lead to changed negotiating behavior and thus lead to a weakening of these social and environmental frameworks from other directions.

To return to private regulation, industry-wide regulation is a very promising avenue to be improved. Transferring the subject matter and the industry actors into a negotiating arena with enforcement agencies would need to be a step forward in order to give this approach more clout and bite. The main advantage of this approach is that it can bypass the difficulties between developed and developing countries and avoid the competitive advantage situation between developing countries. These are problems that cannot be resolved from the inside of developing countries but cannot be resolved from the global perspective in a neoliberal framework either. The industries involved as the main link between developed and developing countries but also as the users of cheap labor in developing countries are the main point of pressure for change. Therefore any global approach at solving these problems needs to have industrial actors onboard and have them involved in the procedure. By putting an enforcement agent in the form of an international organization and governmental actors in charge of the policy framework, the drawbacks of private initiatives such as codes of conduct and their lack of enforcement are avoided.

Overall, the global approach to solving problems at the local level is clearly limited but on the other hand also clearly necessary. It is paramount to understand that global frameworks can only have a limited role and impact and that these policy tools can only work in conjunction with other approaches. However, at the same time local approaches cannot be successful without stressing the global perspective. Thus the global framework is not the be all and end all but rather one piece in the mosaic of global relations.

GLOBAL GOVERNANCE II:
REGULATING THE GLOBAL THROUGH THE LOCAL

Global problems can also be targeted with local policy options that do indeed often have a wider impact than just in their own locality. Again, a distinction can be made between institutional frameworks at the political and economic level as well as socio-cultural phenomena or institutions that influence policy and behavior.

Some of the institutional local regulatory tools have already been discussed in this book. To recap, for example, European Union (EU) regulations governing the toxicity of dyes in textiles do have a global impact as producers outside the EU want continued access to this market and will therefore comply with these regulations if it becomes necessary. Thus, product standards in developed countries can have an impact globally through sheer market power. This power can be harnessed in several ways.

Stronger consumer protection legislation in industrialized countries can be used to improve the levels of toxins, pesticides, etc in goods produced all over the world but mostly consumed in industrialized countries. Although this method cannot improve conditions of production in developing countries or indeed anywhere else, it can at least improve health and safety conditions by reducing exposure to toxins for workers involved in the production process. This is of social and environmental benefit. This is a social and environmental management solution to environmental and social problems but could become a more structural measure if these measures are sufficiently strict and not watered down by industry-government compromises that do not take account of health and environmental concerns. Thus such a policy option can become a structural issue if environmental and health necessity is put over institutional feasibility.

A serious problem with this point is the compatibility with WTO trade rules. Product standards can seriously impede free trade in that they can be and often are classified as protectionist. In existing cases product standards may well have been used to disguise protectionism but in many cases they are based on different political cultures that accounts for many of the U.S.-EU disputes on hormones in livestock or the state of genetically modified (GM) food to name but two. Usually, the accusation of protectionism is levied against the users of product standards because it implies market restrictions. Thus product standards and the WTO are not necessarily compatible unless the WTO is reformed sufficiently to move away from an absolute emphasis on free trade to an emphasis on free and fair as well as environmentally benign trade. Again, such an approach could be taken from a management perspective or from a more structural basis. However, such structural reform of the WTO—if done rigorously and really lifting equity and environmental as well as social considerations to equal status to economic growth—could have far-reaching consequences and make a difference. This, however, is more of a global rather than local policy tool although the use of regional product standards obviously is not.

A local environmental policy tool with global outreach would be a move toward less trade in agriculture or in other perishable goods or like goods as these lead to increased transport cost and emissions as well as to the increased use of environmental space. Apples from New Zealand in Europe or the transport of cheese across the continent is not an environmentally viable economic option. This is not to argue against trade in agriculture per se that can be extremely beneficial for all parties (e.g., as bananas for the exporting countries and as winter food for vitamin-deficient areas) and certainly not against trade in technological goods as limited trade in these fields would have devastating consequences for developing countries. Rather, limited trade based on necessity rather than on choice of goods would make more environmental sense and not deprive consumers of products from other areas because it would focus on trading what the other trading partner does not possess rather than trading like with like. Thus I argue here for a modification of the law of competitive advantage to take into consideration need and not just efficiency. As this is a global as well as local trade issue, this would have repercussions for the WTO framework as much as on the local level. Again, this is an environmental management as well as a more structural tool depending on how it is used. It does not go to the root of the inequality between developed and developing countries. This root cause will be the subject of the following section and will be highlighted from different angles.

The situation in West Africa in agricultural trade is a case in point. For example, rice imports from Thailand are cheaper in the Burkinabé markets than the local product due to export subsidies granted by the Thai government. Thus local producers are being squeezed out of the market and this has serious implications for issues of social justice and rural poverty. The same problem applies to other produce as well. As long as agricultural subsidies distort the market, it makes no sense to have a free market as it will not lead to the advantages promised by neoliberal ideology. However, normative questions also need to be raised as to whether there should be free markets in agriculture at all. The impetus for change in these agricultural patterns will have to come from the regions most adversely affected. A regrouping of West African governments has recently begun in this subject area.

The root cause of structural inequality between North and South is the unequal distribution of resources and capital. This leads to inequality in human resources and capital as well as to a centralization of power. One aspect of this inequality is the one-sided flow of resources in terms of consumption. Unsustainable consumption patterns in the North lead to unsustainable and inequitable production patterns in the North and South. This unsustainable consumption pattern is fueled by a manic preoccupation with fashion and ever-changing consumable items as well as upgrades in the technological field. Changing socio-cultural norms in the developed world would actually be an extremely strong policy/behavioral measure that could have vast impact globally. In the textile sector for example, a move toward sustained, less fashion-driven, ethical consumption would have a huge impact on production patterns in the developing world. This would obviously lead to higher prices and less disposable income but also to a direct redistribution of wealth.

The importance of consumer power has often been discussed although the consumer as a political agent and even less as an international actor has not been a major analytical unit. In a realist and/or liberal framework the consumer does not figure as an international actor because of the focus on institutional frameworks and in the Marxist framework the consumer is seen as the end product of the production process rather than as an independent social agent. However, consumption as a social institution and thus by extension the consumer as a social agent or even international actor are vital ingredients of the global political economy and even more so of the dynamics perpetuating the gulf between core and periphery. This would necessitate putting on an equal level the issue of consumption, equity, and distributive justice with economic growth concerns by Western governments.

Such a value change would obviously need to be based on a general value change that includes governments and all aspects of civil society-economic and non-economic. This leads back to questions of structure and agency as such far-reaching structural change would obviously need to be initiated by some form of agency. The anti-globalization, or countercapitalist (as the Financial Times refers to it) movement is one agent of change that seems to have a sizable influence on society, albeit not the mainstream. However, in order to harness this form of change, it needs to be an analytical entity first that can then be institutionalized. As such it needs to become a recognized structural, institutional as well as a politico-economic social force. Thus the agency and institution of consumption with the emphasis on fashion is a major local and also regional tool for changing the global.

These points show that the regulation of policy is far from just an institutional and management issue. Although some policy changes are the inclusion of different actors in attempts to deal with a problem that can be very successful, structural change needs to go much further than simply changing a few regulations or institutional agendas. Structural change is related to changing priorities or giving equal status in political, social, economic, and cultural frameworks to problems of equity, environmental protection, and social justice. Although these issues are enshrined in existing international and national law and are part of all societal norms, in international policy-making and social organization they are subordinated to economic growth concerns and liberal values. They are only incorporated within a liberal framework that gives priority to the politico-economic tenets of liberalism. However, it is not the liberalism that needs to be abolished but the anchoring of individual and economic rights in the notion of property and how the accumulation of wealth as a rational pursuit does not take account of equity. In addition, there is no basis for understanding the dependence of society on environmental well-being. A more humane form of liberalism as favored by many social-liberal thinkers offers more scope for reform than the neoliberal model. Such an endeavor can only be achieved through the combined use of social and institutional reform both at the local and global level with the combined use of all actors in the international and global systems.

Bibliography

Adam, B. 1990. Time and Social Theory. London: Polity Press.

Adam, B. 1998. Timescapes of modernity. London: Routledge.

Adam, B. & Kütting, G. 1995. Time to Reconceptualise 'Green Technology' in the Context of Globalisation and International Relations. Innovation—The European Journal of Social Sciences, 8 (3), 243-259.

Adamy, W. 1996. Ein Minimum an Fair Play. Politische Ökologie, 14(45), 54.

Aggarwal, V. 1985. Liberal Protectionism—The International Politics of Organized Textile Trade. Berkeley: University of California Press.

Agnew, J.C. 1993. Coming up for air: consumer culture in historical perspective. In Consumption and the world of goods, eds. J. Brewer & R. Porter. London: Routledge, 19–39.

Allott, P. 2000. Globalization from Above. Review of International Studies 26 (Special Issue), 61–80.

Altvater, E. 1993. The Future of the Market: an essay on the regulation of money and nature after the collapse of 'actually existing socialism'. London: Verso.

Altvater, E & Mahnkopf, B. 1999. Grenzen der Globalisierung; Ökonomie, Ökologie und Politik in der Weltgesellschaft. 4th ed. Münster, Germany: Westfälisches Dampfboot.

Amelrooy, M. van. 1994. Indian environmental policy and the use of economic instruments. Indian Council of Social Science Research. Indo Dutch programme on alternatives in development. Occasional Papers and Reprints No. IDPAD 1994-1.

Anderson, K. 1992. New Silk Roads: East Asia and World Textile Markets. Cambridge: Cambridge University Press.

Anon. 2000. Endosulfan deaths in Benin. Pesticides News (March), 74.

Anon. 2001. Cotton Pesticides Cause More Deaths in Benin. Pesticides News (June), 52.

Aryeetey E. & Oduso A. 1996. Regional Integration Efforts in Africa: An Overview In. Teunissen JJ, Regionalism and the Global Economy: The Case of Africa, FONDAD. Netherlands: The Hague.

Armstrong, D. 1998. Globalization and the Social State. Review of International Studies 24(4), 461-478.

Arntzen, J. Hemmer, I., & Kuik, O., eds. 1992. International Trade and Sustainable Development. Amsterdam: VU University Press.

Asante, S. 1996. Comment on Aryeetey E. & Oduso A. 1996. Regional Integration Efforts in Africa: An Overview In. Teunissen JJ, Regionalism and the Global Economy: The Case of Africa, FONDAD. Netherlands: The Haguel.

Axtmann, R. 1996. Liberal democracy into the twenty-first century; globalization, integration and the nation-state. Manchester University Press, Manchester.

Bagchi, S. 1994. The integration of the textile trade into GATT. Journal of World Trade 28(6), 31–42.

Balaam, D. & Veseth, M. 1996. Introduction to International Political Economy. Upper Saddle River, NJ: Prentice Hall.

Bantenga, M. W. 2000. Etude Sur La Filière Coton. Oxfam Report on Microecomic Aspects of West African Cotton Chain, Dakar/Senegal.

Banuri, T. 1998. Global Product Chains: Northern Consumers, Southern Producers and Sustainability—Cotton and Textiles in Pakistan. Prepared for United Nations Environment Programme.

Barber, E. W. 1994. Women's Work: The First 20,000 Years. New York: Norton.

Barnett, B. & Gibson, B. 1999. Economic Challenges of Transgenic Crops: The Case of BT Cotton. Journal of Economic Issues 33(3), 647–659.

Baudrillard, J. 1998. The Consumer Society; Myth and Structure. Translated by George Ritzer. Originally published in 1970 as La Société de Consommation ed. London: Sage.

Bauman, Z. 1998a. Work, Consumerism and the New Poor. Buckingham: Open University Press.

Bauman, Z. 1998b. Globalization, the Human Consequences. London: Polity Press.

Beaumont, P. 1993. Pesticides, Policies and People. London: Pesticides Trust.

Bergesen, A. & Parisi, L. 1999. Ecosociology and Toxic Emissions. In Ecology and The World System, eds. W. Goldfrank, D. Goodman, A. Szasz. London: Greenwood, 43–57.

Berkhout, F. 1997. Life Cycle Assessment and Industrial Innovation. ESRC GEC Programme Briefing No. 14.

Berlanga-Albrecht, L. 1999. Japanese Maquiladoras in Tijuana, Mexico: Productive structure and global input chains. Paper presented at the 1999 ISA Conference, Washington DC.

Bernstein, S. 2001. The Compromise of Liberal Environmentalism. New York: Columbia University Press.

Birchfield, V. 1999. Contesting the Hegemony of Market Ideology: Gramsci's 'Good Sense' and Polanyi's 'Double Movement.' Review of International Political Economy 6(1), 27–54.

Blokker, N. & Deelstra, J. 1994. Towards a Termination of the Multi-Fibre Arrangement? Journal of World Trade 28(5), 97–118.

Boris, J. P. 2002. Cotton: Sentenced to death. Faced with American producers, strongly subsidised, the African farmers are outrageously unprotected. www.abcburkina.net (October 2001).

Boyer, R. & Drache, D. eds. 1996. States Against Markets—the Limits of Globalization. London: Routledge.

Brah, A., Hickman, M. & Mac an Ghaill, M. eds. 1999. Global Futures—Migration, Environment and Globalisation. Basingstoke, UK: Macmillan.

Brandt, H. 1989. Die Baumwollerzeugung Afrikanischer Länder, Internationale Wettbewerbsfähigkeit und Ökologische Probleme. Deutsches Institut für Entwicklungspolitik, Schriften Nr. 97.

Brassel, F. 1996. Etikettenschwindel. Politische Ökologie 14(45), 55.

Braudel, F. 1993. A History of Civilizations. London: Penguin.

Brett, E. A. 1997. A Case for Structural Adjustment. New Political Economy 2(2), 322–325.

Brewer, J. & Porter, R. eds. 1993. Consumption and the World of Goods. London: Routledge.

Bryner, G. 2001. Gaia's Wager; Environmental Movements and the Challenge of Sustainability. New York: Rowman & Littlefield.

BUND 1999. Positionspapier. Internal Discussion Paper of Textile Group of German NGO.

Bunker, S. G. & Ciccantell, P. S. 1999. Economic Ascent and the Global Environment: World-Systems Theory and the New Historical Materialism. In: Ecology and the World System. Eds. W. Goldfrank, D. Goodman, & A. Szasz. London: Greenwood Press, 107–122.

CAFOD, Green, D. & Jones, L. 1998. The Asian Garment Industry and Globalisation. CAFOD Report.

Camilleri, J. 1996. Impoverishment and the National State. In Earthly Goods, Environmental Change and Social Justice, Eds. F. O. Hampson & J. Reppy. Ithaca NY: Cornell University Press, 122–153.

Campbell, C. 1987. The Romantic Ethic and the Spirit of Modern Consumerism. London: Blackwell Publishers.

Carr, S. J. 1993. Improving Cash Crops in Africa: Factors Influencing the Productivity of Cotton, Coffee and Tea Grown by Smallholders. World Bank Technical Paper No. 216.

Castro, A. P. 1998. Sustainable Agriculture or Sustained Error? The Case of Cotton in Kirinyaga, Kenya. World Development 26(9), 1719–1731.

Cavanagh, J. 1997. The Global Resistance to Sweatshops. In: No sweat, Ed. A. Ross. London: Verso, 39–50.

Cerny, P. 1998. Embedding Global Finance: Markets as Governance Structures. Paper Presented at BISA Annual Conference, Brighton, December 1998.

Chadhuri, K. N. 1990. Asia before Europe: Economy and Civilization of the Indian Ocean from the Rise of Islam to 1750. Cambridge, UK: Cambridge University Press.

Chazan, N. et. al. 1999. Politics and Society in Contemporary Society. 3rd ed. Boulder CO: Lynne Rienner.

Cheng, L. 1999. Globalisation and Women's Paid Labour in Asia. International Social Science Journal 41(2), 217–228.

Chew, S. 2000. Ecology in Command. Paper presented at the ISA Annual Convention, Los Angeles, March 2000.

Chew, S. C. 2001. World Ecological Degradation; Accumulation, Urbanization and Deforestation 3000 BC–AD 2000. Walnut Creek CA: Altamira.

Chomsky, N. 1998. Free Trade and Free Markets: Pretense and Practice. In: The Cultures of Globalization, eds. F. Jameson & M. Miyoshi. London: Duke University Press, 356–370.

Chossudovsky, M. 1997. The Globalization of Poverty. London: Zed Books.

Clairmonte, F. & Cavanagh, J. 1981. The World in Their Web; Dynamics of Textile Multinationals. London: Zed Books.

Clapp, J. 1997. Threats to the Environment in an Era of Globalization: An End to State Sovereignty? In: Surviving Globalism, ed. T. Schrecker. Basingstoke, UK: Macmillan, 123–140.

Clapp, J. 2001. Toxic Exports, the Transfer of Hazardous Wastes from Rich to Poor Countries. Ithaca NY: Cornell University Press.

Clark, I. 1998. Beyond the Great Divide: Globalization and the Theory of International Relations. Review of International Studies 24(4), 479–498.

Claus, F. & Völkle, E. 1996. Viele Köche Verderben den Brei. Politische Ökologie 14(45), 31–35.

Collier, A. 1994. Value, Rationality and the Environment. Radical Philosophy 66, 3–9.

Comor, E. 1998. Consumption in the Global Political Economy: Conceptualizing Consumption as an Institution. ISA Annual Conference Paper, Minneapolis.

Conca, K. 2000. The WTO and the Undermining of Global Environmental Governance. Review of International Political Economy 7(3), 484–494.

Conca, K. 2001. Consumption and Environment in a Global Economy. Global Environmental Politics 1(3), 53–71.

Conca, K., Princen, T. & Maniates, M. 2001. Confronting Consumption. Global Environmental Politics 1(3), 1–10.

Conférence des Ministres de l'Agriculture de l'Afrique de l'Ouest et du Centre (CMA/AOC) (2000): Symposium sur l'avenir de la Filière Coton en Afrique de l'Ouest et du Centre. Ouagadougou/Burkina Faso, Ministerial meeting on the future of cotton.

Conley, V. A. 1997. Ecopolitics; The Environment in Poststructuralist Thought. London: Routledge.

Cortes, C. J. 1997. GATT, WTO and the Regulation of International Trade in Textiles. Aldershot, UK: Ashgate Dartmouth.

Cox, R. 1987. Production, Power and World Order: Social Forces in the Making of History. New York: Columbia University Press.

Cox, R. 1996. Approaches to World Order. Cambridge: Cambridge University Press.

Cox, R. 1997. A perspective on Globalisation. In Globalisation, Critical Reflections, ed. J. H. Mittelman. London: Lynne Rienner, 21–33.

Cox, R. ed. 1997. The New Realism—Perspectives on Multilateralism and World Order. Basingstoke, UK: Macmillan.

Cox, R. 1999. Civil Society at the Turn of the Millennium: Prospects for an Alternative World Order. Review of International Studies 25(1), 3–28.

Cox, R. 2000. Thinking about Civilizations. Review of International Studies 26 (Special Issue), 217–233.

Cox, R. W. 1996. Civilizations in World Political Economy. New Political Economy 1(2), 141–156.

Cronon, W. ed. 1996. Uncommon Ground—Rethinking the Human Place in Nature. New York: W.W. Norton & Co.

Cronon, W. 1996. The Trouble with Wilderness; or, Getting Back to the Wrong Nature. In Uncommon Ground—Rethinking the Human Place in Nature, ed. W. Cronon. New York: W.W. Norton & Co., 69–90.

Cullet, P. 2002. Desertification. Entry 1.44.2.6, Unesco Encyclopaedia of Life Support Systems.

Culpeper, R., Berry, A. & Stewart, F. eds. 1997. Global Development Fifty Years After Bretton Woods. Basingstoke, UK: Macmillan.

Cutler, C. 1997. Locating 'Authority' in the International System. Paper presented at the BISA Annual Conference, Leeds, December 1997.

Daly, H. 1996. Beyond Growth—The Economics of sustainable development. Boston: Beacon Press.

Das, S. 1997. The Textiles Trade. Expert Panel on Trade and Sustainable Development Report.

Dasgupta, B. 1998. Structural Adjustment, Global Trade and the New Political Economy of Development. London: Zed Books.

Dauvergne, P. 2000. Loggers and Degradation in the Asia-Pacific. Cambridge, UK: Cambridge University Press.

Davies, I. 1998. Negotiating African Culture: Toward a Decolonisation of the Fetish. In The Cultures of Globalization, eds. F. Jameson & M. Miyoshi. London: Duke University Press, 125–145.

Dembélé, E. 1998. Expérience de la Compagnie Malienne de Développement des Textiles dans la Réalisation des Soles Fourragères Pluriannuelles. www.idrc.ca/books/focus/852/21-sec18.html.

Denemark, R. 1999. World System History: From Traditional International Politics to the Study of Global Relations. International Studies Review 1(2), 43–76.

Denemark, R., Friedman, J., Gills, B. K, & Modelski, G. eds. 2000. World System History, the Social Science of Long Term Change. London: Routledge.

Der Derian, J. 1992. Antidiplomacy, Spies, Terror, Speed and War. Oxford: Blackwell.

Diallo, S. 2002. Le Ministère de l'agriculture de Burkina Faso s'exprime sur la Filière Coton: il Parle de Riposte. www.abcburkina.net (July 16, 2002).

Diawara, M. 1998. Toward a Regional Imaginary in Africa. In The Cultures of Globalization, eds. F. Jameson & M. Miyoshi. London: Duke University Press, 103–124.

Dicken, P. 1992. Global Shift, the Internationalisation of Economic Activity. 2d ed. London: Paul Chapman Publishing.

Diehl, P. & Gleditsch, N. P. 2001. Environmental Conflict. Boulder CO: Westview.

Dobson, A. 1990. Green Political Thought. 2d ed. London: Routledge.

Dodge, B. 1984. Cotton, the Plant that Would be King. Austin: University of Texas Press.

Dorward, A., Kydd, J. & Poulton, C. eds. 1998. Smallholder Cash Crop Production under Market Liberalization. Oxford: CAB International.

Doyle, T. 1998. Sustainable Development and Agenda 21: The Secular Bible of Global Free Markets and Pluralist Democracy. Third World Quarterly 19(4), 771–786.

Drezner, D. 2001. Globalization and Policy Convergence. International Studies Review 3(1), 53–78.

Driver, T. S. & Chapman, G. P. 1996. Timescales and Environmental Change. London: Routledge.

Dryzek, J. 1987. Rational Ecology, Environment and Political Economy. Oxford: Blackwell.

Dryzek, J. 1997. The Politics of the Earth, Environmental Discourses. Oxford: Oxford University Press.

Dussel, E. 1998. Beyond Eurocentrism: The World-System and the Limits of Modernity. In The Cultures of Globalization, eds. F. Jameson & M. Miyoshi. London: Duke University Press, 3–31.

Eckersley, R. ed. 1995. Markets, the State and the Environment. London: Routledge.
Eisa, H. M., Barghouti, S., Gilham, F. & Al-Saffy, M. T. 1994. Cotton Production Prospects for the Decade to 2005. World Bank Technical Paper Number 231.
Elson, D. 1994. Uneven Development and the Textiles and Clothing Industry. In Capitalism and Development, ed. L. Sklair. London: Routledge, 189–210.
Elumalai, K. et al. 1996. Cooperatives: Policy and Environment. The Administrator 41(4), 1–159.
Escobar, A. 1996. Constructing Nature. In: Liberation Ecologies—Environment, Development, Social Movements, eds. R. Peet, & M. Watts. New York: Routledge, 46–68.
ESRC Global Environmental Change Programme (November 2001): Special Briefing No. 7. Environmental Justice, Rights and Means to a Healthy Environment for All.
Evcimen, G., Kaytaz, M. & Mine Cinar, E. 1991. Subcontracting, Growth and Capital Accumulation in Small-Scale Firms in the Textile Industry in Turkey. Journal of Development Studies 28(1), 130–149.
Farah, J. 1994. Pesticide Policies in Developing Countries—Do They Encourage Excessive Use? World Bank Discussion Paper No. 238.
Fayomi, B., Lafia, E., Fourn, L., Akpona, S., Forget, G. & Zohoun, T. 1998. Knowledge and Behaviour of Pesticide Users in Benin. African Newsletter 8(2), 21–33.
Featherstone, M. 1991. Consumer Culture and Postmodernism. London: Sage.
Ferry, L. 1995. The New Ecological Order. University of Chicago Press, Chicago.
Financial Times, 30 January 2002 and 16 October 2001.
Fletcher, K. et al. 1999. Creating a Final Product In Organic Cotton, eds. D. Myers & S. Stolton. London: Intermediate Technology Productions.
Food and Agriculture Organization. Commodities and Trade Division (1992): World apparel fibre consumption survey 1987–1990. ESC/M/93/5.
Fox, J. A. & Brown, D. L. eds. 1998. The Struggle for Accountability. Cambridge MA: Massechusetts Institute of Technology Press.
Fox, M. W. 2001. Bringing Life to Ethics; Global Bioethics for a Humane Society. New York: State University of New York Press.
Frank, A. G. 1998. ReOrient, Global Economy in the Asian Age. London: University of California Press.
Friends of the Earth Middle East 2000. Euro-Mediterranean Free Trade Zone—Implications for Sustainability. Draft Study, Amman/Jerusalem.
Fürst, E. 1999. Globaler Ressourcenverbrauch, Umweltraum und Ökologischer Strukturwandel—Implikationen für die Nord-Süd-Beziehungen. In Globalisierung und Ökologische Krise, eds. W. Hein & P. Fuchs. Hamburg: Deutsches Übersee-Institut, 77–124.
Funke, O. 1997. Biotechnology and Patent Rights: Seeking the Common Good? In: Surviving Globalism, ed. T. Schrecker. Basingstoke, UK: Macmillan, 214–238.
George, S. 1994. A Fate Worse than Debt. London: Penguin.
Gereffi, G. 1996. Commodity Chains and Regional Divisions of Labour in East Asia. Journal of Asian Business 12(1), 75–112.
Gereffi, G. & Korzeniewicz, M. eds. 1994. Commodity Chains and Global Capitalism. London: Praeger.
Gereffi, G., Korzeniewicz, M. & Korzeniewicz, R. 1994. Introduction: Global Commodity Chains. In: Commodity Chains and Global Capitalism, eds. G. Gereffi & M. Korzeniewicz. London: Praeger, 1–14.

Germanwatch 1997. Zukunftsfähiger Handel—Grundlagen für Eine Neue Europäische Handelspolitik. Bonn Tradewatch Nord-Süd Initiative.

Gibbon, P. 1999. Free Competition without Sustainable Development? Tanzanian Cotton Sector Liberalization 1994/5 to 1997/8. Journal of Development Studies 36(1), 128–150.

Giddens, A. 1990. The Consequences of Modernity. Stanford: Stanford University Press.

Gill, S. ed. 1993. Gramsci, Historical Materialism and International Relations. Cambridge: Cambridge University Press.

Gill, S. & Law, D. 1988. The Global Political Economy—Perspectives, Problems and Policies. Hemel Hempstead, UK: Harvester Wheatsheaf.

Gill, S. & Mittelman, J. eds. 1997. Innovation and Transformation in International Studies. Cambridge: Cambridge University Press.

Gillham, F. M. et al. 1995. Cotton Production Prospects for the Next Decade. World Bank technical paper No. 287.

Gills, B. K. 2000. World System Analysis, Historical Sociology and International Relations: The Difference a Hyphen Makes. Paper presented at the ISA Annual Convention, Los Angeles, March 2000.

Gilpin, R. 1987. The political Economy of International Relations. Princeton, NJ: Princeton University Press.

Global Coalition for Africa 2001. 2001/2002 Annual Report. The Private Sector—The Missing Link in African Development Strategies?

Glucksmann, M. 2000. Cottons and Casuals, the Gendered Organization of Labour in Time and Space. Durham, UK: sociologypress.

Goerg, C. & Brand, U. 2000. Global Environmental Politics and Competition Between Nation-States: On the Regulation of Biodiversity. Review of International Political Economy 7(3), 371–398.

Goldfrank, W., Goodman, D. & Szasz, A. eds. 1999. Ecology and the World System. London: Greenwood Press.

Goldman, M. ed. 1998. Privatizing Nature. New Brunswick: Rutgers University Press.

Goodman, D. & Redclift, M. 1991. Refashioning Nature: Food, Ecology & Culture. London: Routledge.

Griffiths, I. 1995. The African Inheritance. London: Routledge.

Guha, R. & Martinez-Alier, J. 1997. From Political Economy to Political Ecology. In: Varieties of Environmentalism; Essays North and South, eds. R. Guha & J. Martinez-Alier. London: Earthscan, 22–45.

Gwynne, R. 1998. Globalization, Commodity Chains and Fruit Exporting Regions in Chile. Tjidschrift voor Economische en Sociale Geografie 90(2), 211–225.

Haas, P. M., Keohane, R. O. & Levy, M. A. eds. 1995. Institutions for the Earth. Cambridge, MA: Massechusetts Institute of Technology Press.

Hale, A. 2002. Trade Liberalization in the Garment Industry: Who is Really Benefitting? Development in Practice 12(1), 33–44.

Halperin, S. 1997. In the Mirror of the Third World. New York: Cornell University Press.

Hampson, F. O. & J. Reppy eds. 1996. Earthly Goods, Environmental Change and Social Justice. Ithaca, NY: Cornell University Press.

Hansen, K. T. 1999. Second-hand Clothing Encounters in Zambia: Global Discourses, Western Commodities and Local Histories. Africa 69(3), 343–365.

Hardin, G. 1968. The Tragedy of the Commons. Science 162(3859), 1234–1238.

Harris, J. ed. 2001. Rethinking Sustainability. Ann Arbor: Michigan University Press.

Harris, P. G. 2001. International Equity and Global Environmental Politics. London: Ashgate.

Harrison, G. 2001. Administering Market Friendly Growth? Liberal Populism and the World Bank's Involvement in Administrative Reform in sub-Saharan Africa. Review of International Political Economy 8(3), 528–547.

Harvey, D. 1998.: What's Green and Makes the Environment Go Round? In: The Cultures of Globalization, eds. F. Jameson & M. Miyoshi. London: Duke University Press, 327–355.

Hay, C. 2000. Contemporary Capitalism, Globalization, Regionalization and the Persistence of National Variation. Review of International Studies 26(4), 509–532.

Heger, E. 1996. Eine Frage der Perspektive. Politische Ökologie 14(45), 45–48.

Hein, W. 1998. Unterentwicklung, Krise der Peripherie. Leske & Budrich, Opladen/Germany.

Hein, W. & Fuchs, P. eds. 199. Globalisierung und Ökologische Krise. Hamburg: Deutsches Übersee-Institut.

Held, D., McGrew, A., Goldblatt, D. & Perraton, J. 1999. Global Transformations. London: Polity Press.

Helleiner, E. 2000. Think Globally, Transact Locally: Green Political Economy and the Local Currency Movement. Global Society 14(1), 35–52.

Helm, C. 1996. Wege in Eine Bessere Zukunft. Politische Ökologie 14(45), 56–59.

Hemmer, I. 1992. The State of the Art: A Critical Review of the Literature. In International Trade and Sustainable Development, eds. J. Arntzen., I. Hemmer, & O. Kuik. Amsterdam: VU University Press, 17–55.

Hertel, T. W. 1996. Growth, Globalisation and the Gains from the Uruguay Round. World Bank research working paper, 1614, Washington DC.

Hewson, M. & Sinclair, T. eds. 1999. Approaches to Global Governance Theory. New York: State University of New York Press.

Higgott, R. 2000. Contested Globalization. Review of International Studies 26(Special Issue), 131–154.

Hines, C. 2000. Localization—A Global Manifesto. London: Earthscan

Hirst, P. & Thompson, G. 1996. Globalization in Question. London: Polity Press.

Hoogvelt, A. 1997. Debate: The African Crisis. New Political Economy 2(2), 317–318.

Hoogvelt, A. 1997. Globalization and the Postcolonial World. Basingstoke, UK: Macmillan.

Hopkins, T. & Wallerstein, I. 1986. World-Systems Analysis: Theory and Methodology, Beverly Hills, CA: Sage.

Hornborg, A. 1998. Ecosystems and World Systems: Accumulation as an Ecological Process. Journal of World-Systems Research 4(2), 169–177.

Hütz-Adams, F. 1996. Ex und Hopp. Politische Ökologie 14(45), 23–25.

IMF Public Information Notices, IMF, Washington DC.

Isaacman, A. 1996. Cotton is the Mother of Poverty. Portsmouth, NH: Heinemann.

Isaacman, A. & Roberts, R. eds. 1995. Cotton, Colonialism and Social History in Sub-Saharan Africa. Portsmouth, NH: Heinemann.

Isaacman, A. & Roberts, R. 1995. Cotton, Colonialism and Social History in Sub-Saharan Africa: Introduction. In Cotton, Colonialism and Social History in Sub-Saharan Africa, eds. A. Isaacman & R. Roberts. Portsmouth, NH: Heinemann, 1–42.

Jameson, F. & Miyoshi, M. eds. 1998. The Cultures of Globalization. London: Duke University Press.

Janelle, D. 1997. Alienation and Globalization. In Surviving Globalism, ed. T. Schrecker. Basingstoke, UK: Macmillan, 38–50.

Jones, R. J. B. 1995. Globalization and Interdependence in the International Political Economy. London: Pinter.

Jordan, G. & Maloney, W. 1997. The Protest Business. Manchester, UK: Manchester University Press.

Kaplinsky, R. 2001. Is Globalization All it is Cracked Up to Be? Review of International Political Economy 8(1), 45–65.

Kathimerini 2001. A Parched Thessaly is Drying Out. 6 July 2001, (English edition)

Keck, M. & Sikkink, K. 1998. Activists Beyond Borders. Ithaca NY: Cornell University Press.

Keohane, R. O. & Levy, M. A. 1996. Institutions for Environmental Aid. Cambridge, MA: Massachussetts Institute of Technology Press.

Kessler, C. 2000. Globalization: Another False Universalism? Third World Quarterly 21(6), 931–942.

Kessler, J. A. 1999. The North American Free Trade Agreement, Emerging Apparel Production Networks and Industrial Upgrading: The Southern California/Mexico Connection. Review of International Political Economy 6(4), 565–608.

Kevane, M. & Englebert, P. 1999. A Developmental State Without Growth. Explaining the Paradox of Burkina Faso in a Comparative Perspective. In African Development Perspectives Yearbook, eds. K. Wohlmuth, H. Bass & F. Messner. Muenster/Germany: Lit Verlag, 259–285.

Klak, T. ed. 1998. Globalization and Neoliberalism; The Caribbean Context. New York: Rowman & Littlefield.

Klein, N. 2000. No logo. London: Flamingo Press.

Knutsen, H. M. 2000. Environmental Practice in the Commodity Chain: The Dyestuff and Tanning Industries Compared. Review of International Political Economy 7(2), 254–288.

Kreissl-Dörfler, W. 1997. Die WTO—Gefahr für Umwelt, Entwicklung und Demokratie? Dossier zur Rolle der EU in der Welthandelsorganisation, Die Grünen im Europäischen Parlament.

Krupat, K. 1997. From War Zone to Free Trade Zone. In No Sweat, ed. A. Ross. New York: Verso, 51–78.

Kütting, G. 2000. Environment, Society and International Relations. London: Routledge.

Laferrière, E. & Stoett, P. 1999. International Relations Theory and Ecological Thought—Towards a Synthesis. London: Routledge.

Langhelle, O. 2000. Sustainable Development and Social Justice: Expanding the Rawlsian Framework of Global Justice. Environmental Values 9(3), 295–323.

Leys, C. 1996. The Rise and Fall of Development Theory. Bloomington, IN: Indiana University Press.

Linnemann, H. & Kox, H. L. M. 1995. International Commodity-related Environmental Agreements as an Instrument for Sustainable Development: Summary Report. Free University of Amsterdam, Department of Development and Agrarian Economics ICREA Research Project.

Lipiètz, A. 1997. The Post-Fordist World: Labour Relations, International Hierarchy and Global Ecology. Review of International Political Economy 4(1), 1–41.

Lipschutz, R. 1999. From Local Knowledge and Practice to Global Environmental Governance. In Approaches to Global Governance Theory, eds. M. Hewson & T. Sinclair. New York: State University of New York Press, 259–283.

Lipschutz, R. 2001a. Environmental History, Political Economy and Change: Frameworks and Tools for Research and Analysis. Global Environmental Politics 1(3), 72–91.

Lipschutz, R. 2001b. Can Social Welfare Policy by Globalized? Reflections on Current Activity and Future Prospects. Paper presented at the ISA Annual Convention, Chicago, February 2001.

Lipschutz, R. & Conca, K. eds. 1993. The State and Social Power in Global Environmental Politics. New York: Columbia University Press.

Lipschutz, R. with Mayer, J. 1996. Global Civil Society and Global Environmental Governance. New York: State University of New York Press.

Litfin, K. ed. 1998. The Greening of Sovereignty in World Politics. Cambridge, MA: Massachusetts Institute of Technology Press.

Little, P. E. 1999. Environments and Environmentalisms in Anthropological Research: Facing a New Millennium. Annual Review of Anthropology 28, 253–284.

Low, N. & Gleeson, B. 1998. Justice, Society and Nature. London: Routledge.

Lukes, S. 1974. Power, A Radical View. Basingstoke, UK: Macmillan.

Maniates, M. 2001. Individualization: Plant a Tree, Buy a Bike, Save the World. Global Environmental Politics 1(3), 31–52.

Martinez-Alier, J. 1998. Environmental Justice (local and global). In The Cultures of Globalization, eds. F. Jameson & M. Miyoshi. London: Duke University Press, 312–326.

Mason, M. 1997. Development and Disorder, A History of the Third World since 1945. Hanover NH: University Press of New England.

Massey, D. 1999. Imagining Globalization: Power-Geometrics of Time-Space. In: Global Futures—Migration, Environment and Globalization, eds. A. Brah, M. Hickman, and M. Mac an Ghaill) Basingstoke, UK: Macmillan, 27–44.

McKendrick, N., Brewer, J. & Plum, J. H. 1982. The Birth of a Consumer Society. London: Europa Publications Ltd.

McNeill, J. R. 1992. The Mountains of the Mediterranean World: An Environmental History. Cambridge: Cambridge University Press.

Merchant, C. 1992. Radical Ecology; The Search for a Livable World. London: Routledge.

Michaelowa, A. & Michaelowa, K. 1996. Der Seidene (Handels-)Faden. Politische Oekologie 14(45), 49–53.

Midgley, M. 2000. Individualism and the Concept of Gaia. Review of International Studies 26 (Special Issue), 29–44.

Miles, E. L., Andresen, S., Wettestad, J., Skjaerseth, J. B. & Carlin, E. M. eds. 2002. Environmental Regime Effectiveness, Confronting Theory with Evidence. Cambridge, MA: Massachusetts Institute of Technology Press.

Miles, S. 1998. Consumerism as a Way of Life. London: Sage.

Miller, M. 1994. Intersystemic Discourse and Co-ordinated Dissent: A Critique of Luhmann's Concept of Ecological Communication. Theory, Culture & Society 11(2), 101–121.

Miller, M. 1995. The Third World in Global Environmental Politics. Boulder, CO: Lynne Rienner.

Miller, M. 2001. Tragedy for the Commons: The Enclosure and Commodification of Knowledge. In The International Political Economy of the Environment, Critical Perspectives, eds. D. Stevis & V. Assetto. Boulder, CO: Lynne Rienner, 111–134.

Mintz, S. W. 1985. Sweetness and Power, the Place of Sugar in Modern History. London: Penguin.

Mittelman, J. 2000. The Globalization Syndrome. Princeton, NJ: Princeton University Press.

Mittelman, J. 2002. Globalization: An Ascendant Paradigm? International Studies Perspectives 3(1), 1–13.

Mittelman, J. H. ed. 1997. Globalisation, Critical Reflections. London: Lynne Rienner.

Mol, A. 2001. Globlization and Environmental Reform. Cambridge, MA: Massachusetts Institute of Technology Press.

Mshomba, R. E. 2000. Africa in the Global Economy. Boulder, CO: Lynne Rienner.

Munck, R. & O'Hearn, D. eds. 1999. Critical Development Theory: Contributions to a New Paradigm. London: Zed Books.

Murphy, C. 2001. Political Consequences of the New Inequality. International Studies Quarterly 45(3), 347–356.

Murray, D. L. & Taylor, P. L. 2000. Claim No Easy Victories: Evaluating the Pesticide Industry's Global Safe Use Campaign. World Development 28(10), 1735–1749.

Murray, D. L. 1994. Cultivating Crisis: The Human Cost of Pesticides in Latin America. Austin: University of Texas Press.

Musiolek, B. 2000. Tools for Enforcing Labour Rights and Ensuring Corporate Social Responsibility in the Garment Sector: The South-East European Context. South-East Europe Review 3, 123–136.

Myers, D. & Stolton, S. eds. 1999. Organic Cotton—From Field to Final Product. London: Intermediate Technology Publications Ltd.

Ndegwa, S. 1997. A Case Against Structural Adjustment. New Political Economy 2(2), 318–321.

Newell, P. 2001. Environmental NGOs, TNCs, and the Question of Governance. In The International Political Economy of the Environment; Critical Perspectives, eds. D. Stevis & V. Assetto. Boulder, CO: Lynne Rienner, 85–109.

New Internationalist (1998): The Big Jeans Stitch-up. No. 302, June 1998, special issue on the social and environmental consequences of jeans production.

New Scientist 2002. The Great Globalisation Debate, April 27, pp. 30–50.

Norgaard, R. 1994. Development betrayed. London: Routledge.

Noticias, 19 July 1941.

Nunnenkamp,P (1995): Verschärfte Weltmarktkonkurrenz, Lohndruck und Begrenzte Wirtschaftspolitische Handlungsspielräume-die Textil-und Bekleidungsindustrie im Zeitalter der Globalisierung. Aussenwirtschaft 50(10), 545–569.

O'Brien, R. 2000. Workers and World Order: The Tentative Transformation of the International Union Movement. Review of International Studies 26(4), 533–556.

O'Brien, R., Goetz, A. M., Scholte, J. A, & Williams, M. 2000. Contesting Global Governance, Multilateral Economic Institutions and Global Social Movements. Cambridge: Cambridge University Press.

Pale, F. O. K. 2000. Rapport final de l'atelier de Presentation de la Recherche sur le Coton en Afrique de l'Ouest. Ouagadougou/Burkina Faso, Oxfam Workshop report.

Paterson, M. 1999. Globalization, Ecology and Resistance. New Political Economy 4(1), 129–145.

Paterson, M. 2000. Car Culture and Global Environmental Politics. Review of International Studies 26(2), 253–270.

Pearce, D. & Barbier, E. 2000. Blueprint for a Sustainable Economy. London: Earthscan.

Pearce, D. & Barbier, E. 2001. Blueprint for a Sustainable Economy. London: Earthscan.

Pearce, D., Markadya, A. & Barbier, E. 1989. Blueprint for a Green Economy. London: Earthscan.

Peet, R. & Watts, M. eds. 1996. Liberation Ecologies—Environment, Development, Social Movements. New York: Routledge.

Peet, R. & Watts, M. 1996. Liberation Ecology. In: Liberation Ecologies—Environment, Development, Social Movements, eds. R. Peet & M. Watts. New York: Routledge, 1–45.

Peluso, N. L. & Watts, M. eds. 2001. Violent Environments. Ithaca, NY: Cornell University Press.

Pepper, D. 1993. Eco-socialism—From Deep Ecology to Social Justice. London: Routledge.

Perrons, D. 1999. Reintegrating Production and Consumption or Why Political Economy Still Matters. In Critical Development Theory: Contributions to a New Paradigm, eds. R. Munck & D. O'Hearn. London: Zed Books, 91–112.

Pesticides Trust 1990. King Cotton and the Pest. Briefing paper on Pesticide Use in Cotton, London.

Pesticides Trust (1997–2001): Pesticides News.

Pettman, R. 1996. Understanding International Political Economy with Readings for the Fatigued. Boulder, CO: Lynne Rienner.

Plattner, M. & Smolar, A. eds. 2000. Globalization, Power and Democracy. Baltimore: The Johns Hopkins University Press.

Ponting, C. 1991. A Green History of the World. London: Penguin.

Porter, G., Brown, J. W. & Chasek, P. 2001. Global Environmental Politics, 3rd ed. Boulder, CO: Westview Press.

Porter, P. 1995. Note on Cotton and Climate: A Colonial Conundrum. In Cotton, Colonialism and Social History in Sub-Saharan Africa, eds. A. Isaacman & R. Roberts. Portsmouth, NH: Heinemann, 43–49.

Poulton, C. 1998. Cotton Production and Marketing in Northern Ghana. In Smallholder Cash Crop Production Under Market Liberalization, eds. A. Dorward, J. Kydd & C. Poulton. Oxford: CAB International, 56–112.

Poulton, C., Dorward, A., Kydd, J., Poole, N. & Smith, L. 1998. A New Institutional Economics Perspective on Current Policy Debates. In Smallholder Cash Crop Production Under Market Liberalization, eds. A. Dorward, J. Kydd & C. Poulton. Oxford: CAB International, 8–41.

Prescott-Allen, R. 2001. The Wellbeing of Nations. Island Press, Washington DC.

Princen, T. 2001. Consumption and Its Externalities: Where Economy Meets Ecology. Global Environmental Politics 1(3), 11–30.

Princen, T. & Finger, M. 1994. Environmental NGOs in World Politics. London: Routledge.

Ramesh, M. 1994. Explaining Cross-Industry Variations in Trade Protection: Textiles, Clothing and Footwear in Canada. Review of International Studies 20(1), 75–96.

Redclift, M. 1987. Sustainable Development, Exploring the Contradictions. London: Routledge.

Redclift, M. 1996. Wasted; Counting the Cost of Global Consumption. London: Earthscan.

Reichert, T. 2000. Study on the Cotton Sector in West Africa—Macroeconomic Aspects. Oxfam briefing paper.

Roberts, J. T. & Grimes, P. E. 1999. Extending the World-System to the Whole System: Toward a Political Economy of the Biosphere. In Ecology and the World System, eds. W. Goldfrank, D. Goodman & A. Szasz. London: Greenwood Press, 59–83.

Roberts, R. 1996. Two Worlds of Cotton—Colonialism and the Regional Economy in the French Soudan, 1800–1946. Stanford: Stanford University Press.

Robertson, Roland. 1992. Globalization: Social Theory and Global Culture. London: Sage.

Rodriguez Meza, L. 1997. Testimony. In No Sweat, ed. A. Ross. London: Verso, 4–8.

Rosenau, J. & Czempiel, O. 1992. Governance without Government. Cambridge, UK: Cambridge University Press.

Ross, A. ed. 1997. No Sweat—Fashion, Free Trade and the Rights of Garment Workers. New York: Verso.

Ross, E. B. 1998. The Malthus Factor. London: Zed Books.

Ruggie, J. 1982. International Regimes, Transactions and Change: Embedded Liberalism in the Postwar Economic Order. International Organization 36(2), 379–415.

Ruqiu, Y. & Fengzhong, C. 1998. Integrated Policy Recommendation for Environment and Trade—A Case Study in the Textile Sector of China. Expert Panel on Trade and Sustainable Development report.

Sachs, W., Loske, R. & Linz, M. 1998. Greening the North, a Post-Industrial Blueprint for Ecology and Equity. London: Zed Books.

Sajhau, J. P. 1997. Business Ethics in the Textile, Clothing and Footwear Industries: Codes of Conduct. ILO Sectoral Activities Programme working papers No. 110, SAP2.60/WP.110.

Sawadogo, J. M. 1997. Burkina Faso Protects its Fragile Soils; Environmental Sustainability is Key to Agricultural Revival. Africa Recovery 11(2), 20–24.

Schaeffer, R. 1997. Understanding Globalization—The Social Consequences of Political, Economic and Environmental Change. Lanham/Maryland: Rowman & Littlefield.

Schneidewind, U. & Hummel, J. 1996. Von der Öko-Nische zum Massenmarkt. Politisch Ökologie 14(45), 63–66.

Scholte, J. A. 1993. International Relations of Social Change. Milton Keynes: Open University Press.

Scholte, J. A. 2000. Globalization, A Critical Introduction. Basingstoke, UK: Palgrave.

Schor, J. & Holt, D. eds. 2000. The Consumer Society Reader. New York: The New Press.

Schott, J., ed. 1998. Launching New Global Trade Talks, An Action Agenda. Vol. 12. Washington, DC: Institute for International Economics.

Schott, J. J. ed. 1990. Completing the Uruguay Round. Institute for International Economics, Washington, DC.

Schrader, T. H., Wennink, B. H., Veldkamp, W. J. & Defoer, T. 1998. Natural Resource Management in the Cotton Zone of Southern Mali. In Closing the Loop: From Research on Natural Resources to Policy Change, eds. S. R. Tabor & D. C. Faber. Policy Management Report No. 8, Maastricht European Centre for Development Policy Management, pp. 142–155.

Schrecker, T. ed. 1997. Surviving Globalism—The Social and Environmental Consequences. Basingstoke, UK: Macmillan.

Schwartz, H. 2000. States versus Markets. 2d ed. Basingstoke, UK: Macmillan.

Schweitz, M. 2001. NGO Network Codes of Conduct: Accountability, Principles and Voice. Paper presented at the ISA Annual Convention, Chicago, February 2001.

Sen, A. 1999. Development as Freedom. Oxford: Oxford University Press.

Shaw, M. 2000. Theory of the Global State. Cambridge: Cambridge University Press.

Shue, H. 1996. Environmental Change and the Varieties of Justice. In Earthly Goods, Environmental Change and Social Justice, eds. F. O. Hampson & J. Reppy. Ithaca, NY: Cornell University Press, 9–29.

Singh, G. 1996. Cotton Co-operatives in India. The Administrator 19, 65–77.

Sklair, L. ed. 1994. Capitalism and Development. London: Routledge.

Sklair, L. 1998. Social Movement and Global Capitalism. In The Cultures of Globalization, eds. F. Jameson & M. Miyoshi. London: Duke University Press, 291–311.

Sklair, L. 2002. Globalization, Capitalism and Its Alternatives. Oxford, UK: Oxford University Press.

Solomon, R. 1994. The Transformation of the World Economy. 2d ed. Basingstoke, UK: Macmillan.

Somo—Centre for Research on Multinational Corporations; Rosier, M. 1997. Producers of Sportswear: Company Profiles of Nike, Reebok, Adidas, Puma. Amsterdam, Clean Clothes Campaign.

Somo—Centre for Research on Multinational Corporations; van Eijk, J. & Zeldenrust, I. 1997. Monitoring Working Conditions in the Garment and Sportswear Industry. Amsterdam, Clean Clothes Campaign.

Somo—Centre for Research on Multinational Corporations; Zeldenrust, I. & van Eijk, J. 1992. Clean Clothes—Strategies for the Improvement of the Labour Situation in the Garment Industry from a Consumer Perspective. Amsterdam, Clean Clothes Campaign.

Soth, J. 1999. The Impact of Cotton on Fresh Water Resources and Ecosystems. WWF Background paper.

Spinanger, D. 1998. Textiles Beyond the MFA Phase-Out. Centre for the Study of Globalization and Regionalisation Working Paper, Warwick.

Steinberg, P. 2001. Environmental Leadership in Developing Countries. Cambridge, MA: Massachusetts Institute of Technology Press.

Stevis, D. 2000. Whose Ecological Justice? Strategies 13(1), 63–76.

Stevis, D. & Assetto, V. eds. 2001. The International Political Economy of the Environment. 12th International Political Economy Yearbook ed. Boulder, CO: Lynne Rienner.

Strange, S. 1988. States and Markets. London: Pinter.

Strange, S. 1996. The Retreat of the State. Cambridge: Cambridge University Press.

Strange, S. 1998. Mad Money. Manchester: Manchester University Press.

Sulkunen, P. 1997. Introduction: The New Consumer Society—Rethinking the Social Bond. In: Constructing the New Consumer Society, eds. Sulkunen, P., Holmwood, J., Radner, H., & G. Schulze. Basingstoke, UK: Macmillan, 1–20.

Sulkunen, P., Holmwood, J., Radner, H. & Schulze, G. eds. 1997. Constructing the New Consumer Society. Basingstoke, UK: Macmillan.

Teeple, G. 1997. Globalization as the Triumph of Capitalism: Private Property, Economic Justice and the New World Order. In Surviving Globalism, ed. T. Schrecker. Basingstoke, UK: Macmillan, 15–37.

Teunissen, J. J. ed. 1996. Regionalism and the Global Economy—The Case of Africa. Fondad (Forum on Debt and Development), The Hague.

Thomas, C. 2000. Global Governance, Development and Human Security. London: Pluto Press.

Thomas, C. Wilkin, P. eds. 1997. Globalization and the South. Basingstoke, UK: Macmillan.

Toyne, B. et al. 1984. The Global Textile Industry. London: George Allen & Unwin.

United Nations Conference on Trade and Development (1996): The Uruguay Round and the World Cotton Market: a Preliminary Overview. UNCTAD/COM/77.

United Nations Economic and Social Commission for Western Asia (1997): Trade Policy Aspects of Environmental Measures in the ESCWA Countries. E/ESCWA/ED/1996/4, New York.

van Dijk, M. P. & Sideri, S. eds. 1996. Multilateralism versus Regionalism: Trade Issues after the Uruguay Round. London: Frank Cass.

Virilio, P. 1986. Speed and Politics. Foreign Agents Series. New York: Semiotexte.

Vogel, D. 1997. International Trade and Environmental Regulation. In Environmental Policy in the 1990s. eds. N. Vig & M. Kraft. Congressional Quarterly Inc., Washington DC, 345–364.

Vogler, J & M. Imber, eds. 1996: The Environment and International Relations. London: Routledge.

von Moltke, K. and O. Kuik. 1998. Global Product Chains: Northern Consumers, Southern Producers and Sustainability—Part 1: Global Product Chains and the Environment. Institute for Environmental Studies, Amsterdam, prepared for United Nations Environment Programme.

Walgate, R. 1990. Miracle or Menace? Biotechnology and the Third World. London: The Panos Institute.

Wallace, I. & Knight, D. B. 1996. Societies in Space and Place. In Earthly Goods, eds. F. O. Hampson & J. Reppy. Ithaca, NY: Cornell University Press, 75–95.

Wallerstein, I. 1986. Africa and the Modern World. Africa World Press, Trenton NJ.

Wallerstein, I. 1995. After Liberalism. New York: The New Press.

Wallerstein, I. 1999. Ecology and Capitalist Costs of Production: No Exit. In: Ecology and the World System, eds. W. Goldfrank, D. Goodman, & A. Szasz. London: Greenwood Press, 3–11.

Wapner, P. 1998. Reorienting State Sovereignty: Rights and Responsibilities in the Environmental Age. In The Greening of Sovereignty in World Politics, ed. K. Litfin. Cambridge, MA: Massachusetts Institute of Technology Press, 275–297.

Wapner, P. 2002. The Sovereignty of Nature? Environmental Protection in a Postmodern Age. International Studies Quarterly 46(2), 167–187.

Warner, C. 2001. The Rise of the State System in Africa. Review of International Studies 27(Special Issue), 65–90.

Watts, M. 1983. Silent Violence. Los Angeles: University of California Press.

Weber, C. 1996. Von Wegen Naturfaser . . . Politische Oekologie 14(45), 36–40.

Weber, M. 1930. The Protestant Ethic and the Spirit of Capitalism. London: Unwin.

Weber, M. 2001. Competing Political Visions: WTO Governance and Green Politics. Global Environmental Politics 1(3), 92–113.

Weller, I. 1994. Globalisierung und Chemisierung. Forum Wissenschaft 3/94 (March), 6–10.

Weskamp, C. 1996. Wohin die Reise geht. Politische Oekologie 14(45), 26–28.

Whalley, J & Zissimos, B. 1999. A World Environmental Organization? Centre for the Study of Globalisation and Regionalisation Working Paper, Warwick.

Wiemann, J. 1994. Green Protectionism: A Threat to Third World Exports? In Multilateralism Versus Regionalism: Trade Issues After the Uruguay Round, eds. M. P. van Dijk & S. Sideri. London: Frank Cass, 91–119.

Williams, M. 2001. In Search of Global Standards: The Political Economy of Trade and the Environment. In The International Political Economy of the Environment— Critical Perspectives. 12th International Political Economy Yearbook ed., eds. D. Stevis & V. Assetto. Boulder, CO: Lynne Rienner, 39–62.

Wilson, F. 1991. Sweaters—Gender, Class and Workshop-based Industry in Mexico. Basingstoke, UK: Macmillan.

Wilson, F. 1992. Technology and Workshop-Based Production in Mexico—The Case of the Garment Industry. Centre for Development Research, Working Paper 92/4, Copenhagen.

Wilson, F. & Arias, P. 1995. Clothing, Identity and Consumption in a Mexican Region. Centre for Development Research Working Paper 95.9, Copenhagen.

Windfuhr, M. 1996. Sprungbrett zur Industrialisierung. Politische Ökologie 14(45), 41–44.

Woods, N. ed. 2000. The Political Economy of Globalization. Basingstoke, UK: Macmillan.

World Development Indicators. 2000. World Bank Publications, Washington, DC.

Yang, Y. 1994. The Impact of MFA Phasing Out on World Clothing and Textile Markets. *Journal of Development Studies* 30(4), 892–915.

Young, O. ed. 1997. Global Governance, Drawing Insights from the Environmental Experience. Cambridge MA: Massachusetts Institute of Technology Press.

Interviews:

April 1999.   Oxfam UK, various members of staff.

April 1999.   Pesticides Trust, Dorothy Myers.

August 2002.   UNPCB (Union Nationale des Producteurs de Colon de Burkina Faso), M. François Traoré, Bobo-Dibulasso, Burkiná Faso Sedelan, Père Maurice Oudet, Koudougon/Burkina Faso, cotton farmers in various villages in Burkina Faso.

Index

accumulation, and consumer culture, 94
Adam, B., 32
advertising, and conspicuous consumption, 98
African regions, economic organization, 110–111
agency, and globalization, 19; and the consumer, 62; question of, 72
Agenda 21, pesticide reduction, 104–105
agenda-setting, temporality, 71
Agrochemical sector, power of, 123
American Fiber Manufacturers Association, 103
anthropocentrism, 73
Asante, S., 111
austerity programs, and public debt, 113–114

Banuri, T., 92, 102
Baudrillard, J., 47
Brett, E., 112, 113
Bretton Woods system, 6, 12, 13
Brewer, J., 48
Brundtland Report (1987), 17
Bund für Natur und Umweltschutz Deutschland (BUND), 97

Campbell, C., 48, 94
capital accumulation, 10
capital flight, 70
capitalism, and globalization, 5; and history, 7
capitalist societies, "pre-industrial, pre-modern," 23
cash crops, and disembedded social and cultural institutions, 124; and the slave trade, 108; World Bank and IMF policies, 92

'ceaseless accumulation,' 10
Chew, S., 26
Civil society, 28, 99
civil society, and the cotton chain, 93
codes of conduct, 93
codes of conduct, Nike and Gap, 129
Codex Alimentarius Commission, 104
colonization, West Africa, 108–109
commodity chain, and the social construct of an economy, 51; global, 50
commodity chain analysis, 59; and historical materialist, 50; and world systems approach, 50
commodity chains, networks of labor and production processes, 49
Compaignie Malienne pour le Développement des Textiles, 115
comparative sustainability, 97
competitive advantage, 133; need versus efficiency, 135
competitiveness, and impediments to, 78
Conca, K., 54
consumer, and influence on production, 62; responsibility, 62
consumer class, 53
consumer culture, and accumulation, 94
consumer protection legislation, 134
consumer society, 93
consumerism, and Protestant ethic, 48; and romanticism, 48; and the Industrial Revolution, 49; and the rise of modern capitalism, 48
consumers, and their purchasing choices, 59
Consumption and Equity, 60–61
Consumption, as an Environmental Issue, 55–60

Consumption, Commodity Chains and, 49–52
Consumption, The Global Division of Labor and, 52–55
consumption, an influence on production, 46; and cheap labor, 96; and emotional pleasure, 94; and patterns of, 96; and social bonds, 94; and structural origins, 59; and the consumer ethic, 94; and the environment, 56; as a cultural phenomenon, 44; as a supply and demand variable, 128; 'collusion' of the consumer, 97; "economies of flexibility, fundamental inequalities, patterns of environmental degradation," 47; excluded form political science, 48; "garment, in Europe," 97; households and, 50; marginalization of, 93; the ethic of, 47; tyranny of, 52; ignored in political economy, 46
consumption and production, the primacy of, 45
core-periphery, 6; and cotton, 89
corporate codes of conduct, 37–38
cosmopolitan, or global justice, 76
Cotton and Textiles Today—From Production to Consumption, 91–99
cotton, as a cash crop, 91; demand and consumption, 114; problems of intensive agriculture, 123
cotton dependence, West Africa, 117–118
cotton market, decoupling (local and global), 109–110
cotton processes, 103
cotton production, problems, 121–123
Cotton Sector, West Africa, 114–118
Cox, R., 5, 8, 11, 54
critical and alternative GPE, 19
Cronon, W., 65
cultural identity, 57
culture, problems of definition, 43; reflectivist and post-modern approaches, 45; social construction of the environment, 45; social practices and their influence on belief systems, 44
Culture as Consumption, 45–48

Debt and Structural Adjustment (West Africa), 111–114
Der Derian, James, 34
distanciation, between accumulation of capital and environmental degradation, 30–31; between production and consumption, 30
division of labor, 5; and governments, 67
Drezner, D., 14
Dryzek, J., 67

ecocentrism, 73
eco-holism, and time, 30
eco-holistic, 22; and GPE approach, 23
eco-holistic approach, 43, 52, 125
eco-holistic perspective, 9
eco-holistic political economy, 58, 127
eco-labeling, 105; Blue Angel, 105
ecological time, 30
ecological world systems, and increasing levels of trade, 41; approach, 27
ecological world systems theory, and alternative to historical materialist orthodoxy, 26
ecological world systems theory, 26, 125
economic exporting zones, EEZ, 99; and sweatshops, 99
economic governance, lack of environmental provision, 35
economic rights, 79
ecosocialist, environmental justice, 74
ecosystems, and waste, 17
ECOWAS, Economic Community of West African States, 110
embedded liberalism, 18
empires, decline in natural resources, 26
Englebert, P., 114
enlightenment, 23; and the mastering of nature, 25; philosophy, 59
Environment and Globalization, 28–30

environment, and social relations, 30; and structural adjustment plans, 36; cause and effect relationships, 63; the built or natural environment, 65; and sustainable development, 36; and political economy, 25–28

environmental agreements, lowest common denominator, 40

environmental auditing, 59; change, 65

environmental degradation, 8, 24, 41, 55, 63, 67, 72, 79, 105; and conditions of living, 56; degradation, and human settlements, 32; and structural origins, 27; and technological advances, 27; and wealth creation, 17; and world system formation and decline, 27; as an economic problem, 17; global, 65; natural, 65; social justice and, 58; spread and extent, 125

Environmental Dimension, West Africa, 120–126

Environmental Equity, 69–72

environmental equity, and access to environmental rights, 70; and the socially marginalised, 69; anthropocentric focus, 69

Environmental Ethics, 64–69

environmental ethics, and sustainable development, 73; and social relations, 64; and societies, 64; and the space dependent context, 68; issues of agency and legitimacy, 82

environmental governance, and non-environmental organisations, 35

environmental management, 17, 51–52, 131

environmental norms, 131

environmental political economy, and regime theory, 4; Eurocentric, 25

Environmental Side of Production and its Regulation, 102–105

environment-society relations, 26, 37, 39, 41, 42, 75, 128; and colonialism, 28; and globalizing of social relations, 28; globalization and pluralistic global governance, 38; in

developing countries, 28; in the age of globalization, 28; time-space distanciation, 34

environmental, equity and justice, 57

environmental degradation, examples of, 64

environmental regimes, 17

equity, intergenerational, 64

equity, 71

equity deficit, 78

fashion, and consuming elites, 95; social and cultural dominance, 97

feasibility-necessity dichotomy, 128

Featherstone, M., 94

Fletcher, K., 103

Food and Agriculture Organization, 104

food security, loss of, 90

Fordism, 48–53, 61; increased demand for cotton, 96

foreign direct investment, 58; and global capital ownership, 41

fossil fuel economy, 24, 27, 31, 42, 65

Frank, A. G., 9, 10, 11, 26

free trade, and environment improvement, 40

GATT, 40; and the deregulation of international trade, 40; Uruguay Round, subsidies, 113

General Agreement on Tariffs and Trade (GATT), 513

Gereffi, G., 50

Gills, B., 9, 10, 11, 26

Gleeson, B., 67

global accords, 24

global civil society, 5, 19, 20, 60; development of norms, 35; governance, 3; actors as legitimate agents, 81

global commons, 56

global corporate governance, 37–38

global division of labor, 4, 61, 79, 128; and equity, 70; and power, 77, 78; and spatial distanciation of locations of production and consumption, 52, 54; just in time, 34

global economic governance, and disregard of environment-society relations, 36
global environmental degradation, 23
global environmental movements, and Seattle 1999 Genoa 2001, 19
global environmental norms, 131, 132
Global Governance, 34–39
global governance, and disenfranchising of local control, 42; and equity, 70; and NGO involvement, 81; and radical social organisations, 38; and WTO and UN, 35; changing role of the state, 36; development of norms, 35; global codes of conduct, 35; international or transnational regulation or institutionalization, 34; legitimacy of, 38; privatization of, 81; undermining of the developing state, 37
global institutional frameworks, creation of global norms, 130–131; the UN; WTO; Bretton Woods, 131
global norms, and private institutions, 131
global political economy, and consumption, 72; and economic rights, 79; and equity, 77; and structural constraints, 70; and the social and power relations, 61; of the environment, 26; political and moral rights, 76; second-hand clothing market, 97
global political governance, and disregard of environment-society relations, 36
global textile consumption, 104
global trade liberalization, value-neutral, 15
global trade regimes, 24
globalization, a contested term, 21; a new ecological imperialism, 28; as opposed to internationalization, 5; "coca-colaization," 7; and conflict between states, 21; and increased consumption, 28; and post-Fordism, 4; and the international system, 6; as

a continuous social process, 10; culture, historical and material perspective, 43; environmental problems, 8; exploitation of resources, 28; social problems, 8; social relations of transport & communications, 6; societal revolution, 7; spatial reach or speed of communication, 6; time-space distanciation, 29; and hegemonic approach, 16; critics, 17–22
globalizing economy, and the proliferation of trade, 39
Goodman, D., 33
governance, 24; and the African state, 109
governments, role of, 67
Gramsci, A., 9

Hampson, F. O., 57
Hansen, K., 119
Harrison, G., 93
Hemmer, I., 40
historical materialism, and neo-Gramscians, 9
historical materialists, 8–11; and social relations of production, 9
historical perspective, and the exclusion of the environment, 11
Historical Significance of Cotton, 87–91
holistic approach, 47; to IPE, 120
holism, and political economy, 27
Hoogvelt, A., 17
Hopkins, T., 49
Human Development Index, and West African countries, 110

IMF, debt relief programs, 58
IMF Report, Burkino Faso, 111–112
individualization of environmental responsibility, 58
industrial society, and ecosystems, 31
industry-specific regulation, 132–133
Institute of International Applied Systems Analysis, 81

institutional regulatory tools, 134
International Court of Justice, 19
international environmental agreements, 67; governance, 37
International Labor Organization, 133
International Monetary Fund (IMF), passim
international trade rules, and agriculture, 124
International Union for the Conservation of Nature, 81
Isaacman, A., 89, 90

justice, as a social construct, 72

Kevane, M., 114
Klein, N., 94, 97
Korzeniewicz, M., 50
Korzeniewicz, R., 50
Krupat, K., 100
Kyoto Protocol, 35, 131

legal actors, 81
legitimacy, of civil society actors, 82
Liberal environmentalism, 17
liberal market ideology, and the law of comparative advantage, 39
life cycle analysis (LCA), 51
Limits to Growth, 55
Lipschutz, R., 65, 81
Little, P., 65
local environmental policy, 134
Lóme Convention, 119
Low, N., 67

Maniates, M., 58
market, primacy over welfare agendas, 15
market efficiency, 128
McKendrick, N., 48, 49, 93
mechanical systems, and Newtonian concepts and assumptions, 31
Miles, S., 95
Mittelman, J., 5, 77
mode of accumulation, 8, 27
mode of production, 7, 8, 27

Montreal Protocol, 131
Multi Fiber Agreement (MFA), 78, 93; phasing out, 119
multinational corporations, and self-governance, 37
Multinational Companies, and accountability, 20; and collusion with states, 21; and comparative advantage, 20; disproportionate interest, 15
Murray, F., 103
Myers, D., 103

National Labor Committee (US), 101
nature/environment, privatization of, 28
nature-society relations, 59, 128; and productive and consumptive relations, 25
Ndegwa, S., 113
neo-liberal ideology, and equity, 124–125; and fashion, 96
neoliberalism, 58
new social movements, 20; 1992 Rio summit, 16; and fight against negative effects of globalization, 16; as counter hegemonic bloc, 28
NGOs and new social movements, no official legal role, 16
non-governmental actors, 37
non-governmental organizations, as reformists, 80
non-tariff barriers, 14; and environmental standards, 13; and social and human rights, 13

O'Brien, R., 54
order, and social contracts, 75
organic view, connections and dependent relations of nature, 31

parastatal organizations, and cotton production, 114–115, 124; and education; pesticides, 123
Pearce, D., 56
pesticides, 87; impact on health and the environment, 103
Plumb, J. H., 48

policy process, and global civil society actors, 80

political economy, and culture, 44; of fashion, 95; of textiles, 102; and environmental regulation, 104

political economy of developing countries, debt crisis, 107; global institutional policy, 107

political ideology, and the environment, 74

Ponting, C., 26

post-Fordism, 4, 53, 54; and lack of awareness of ethical and environmental conditions, 54; erosion of human and labor rights, 16; Fordism and labor relations, 10

post-Fordist, 61; and fashion, 95; production, and working conditions, 99

power, global economic institutions, 71

pricing environmental goods, 56

product standards, free trade and protectionism, 134

Production and consumption, the history of, 48–49; dichotomy, 127

public interest, and environmental protection, 68; definition of, 68; market efficiency, 68

public opinion, and social justice or equity, 81

race to the bottom, 54

Rawls, J., 76

Redclift, M., 33

regional economic performance, factors affecting, 117

regional trade organisations, 13

Reppy, J., 57

resistance force, 80

resources, need not want campaign, 56

responsibility, question of, 72

Rio Conference, 105

Rio Summit 1992 and agenda setting, 19

Roberts, R., 89

Robertson, R., 44

Ross, A., 100

scarcity, as supply regulation, 82

Seattle, 102

second-hand clothing markets, 119; access to affordable Western clothing, 120

semi-periphery, 6

social activity, and social environmental rhythms, 30

Social and Ecological Justice, 72–77

social and ecological justice, as western concepts, 72

social change, and environmental change, 75

social forces, and the economic process, 43

social justice, 57; and the global agenda, 81

social justice (or equity), and competition, 77; and core periphery analysis, 74; and structural historical materialism, 74; Western concept, 79

social movements, and large retailers, 93; and the potential of consumer power, 98

social relations, and trade and consumption, 27; of production, 9

social time, 30

Sofitex, 115

Sonapra, 115

species conservation, 64

state, changing role in global economy, 18; guardian of capital and production, 18; sovereign actors, 6

Stevis, D., 73

Stoflom, S., 103

Strange, S., 28

structural adjustment, and trade liberalization, 113

structural adjustment programmes (SAP), 58

Structural Constraints in Practice, 127–130

structural inequality, 128, 135
structure and agency, 9; and anti-globalization (countercapitalist), 136
sustainability, and a finite eco-system, 11
sustainable development, 42; and equal opportunities, 129; and excessive trade, 41
sweatshops, 99–100

Taylor, P., 103
Taylorism, 53
Textiles and Garment Sector, West Africa, 118–120
time, and social relations, 30; different notions of, 32; hegemonic social conceptions, 32
time-space distanciation, 24, 33–34, 65; and causal links, 33; and global-local linkages, 33; and the environment, 32; disconnecting social activity, 33; environment-society relations, 34; social organizations, 34
Trade, 39–41
trade, and an environmental dimension, 39; and governance, 24; and the environment, 24; necessity versus choice, 135
trade agreements, and environmental provision, 42
trade barriers, 13
trade in waste, 70
trade liberalization, 40; and the liberalization of capital and finance, 41; regulation and protected markets, 40
trade liberalization movement, 128
transnational capitalist class, 4
transnational governance, 37

transnational protest movements, 37
tyranny of expectations, 60

UN, and NGO involvement, 80
UN Conference for the Human Environment 1972, 56
United Nations (UN), passim
unlimited economic growth, fallacy of, 59

Virilio, P., 34
voluntary codes, of conduct; of behavior, 38, 129, 132
von Hayek, F., 12

Wallerstein, I., 9, 10, 26, 49
Weber, M., 9, 34
welfare and social frameworks, subordinated to rules of the market, 133
World Bank, and NGO cooperation, 16; environmental policy, 129
World Health Organization, 104
world systems, sociologists, 8; theorists, 8
world systems theory, 89
World Trade Organization (WTO), passim
world trade rules and regulations, and West African countries, 113
WTO, and concept of state sovereignty, 19; and erosion of power, 21; cross-retaliation, 18; dispute resolution, 18; textiles and the relocation of production, 61; and business NGOs, 16
WTO rules, erosion of state sovereignty, 14; higher labor and environmental standards, 14; priority of the market, 14

SUNY series in Global Politics
James N. Rosenau, Editor

LIST OF TITLES

American Patriotism in a Global Society—Betty Jean Craige

The Political Discourse of Anarchy: A Disciplinary History of International Relations—Brian C. Schmidt

From Pirates to Drug Lords: The Post—Cold War Caribbean Security Environment—Michael C. Desch, Jorge I. Dominguez, and Andres Serbin (eds.)

Collective Conflict Management and Changing World Politics—Joseph Lepgold and Thomas G. Weiss (eds.)

Zones of Peace in the Third World: South America and West Africa in Comparative Perspective—Arie M. Kacowicz

Private Authority and International Affairs—A. Claire Cutler, Virginia Haufler, and Tony Porter (eds.)

Harmonizing Europe: Nation-States within the Common Market—Francesco G. Duina

Economic Interdependence in Ukrainian-Russian Relations—Paul J. D'Anieri

Leapfrogging Development? The Political Economy of Telecommunications Restructuring—J. P. Singh

States, Firms, and Power: Successful Sanctions in United States Foreign Policy—George E. Shambaugh

Approaches to Global Governance Theory—Martin Hewson and Timothy J. Sinclair (eds.)

After Authority: War, Peace, and Global Politics in the Twenty-First Century—Ronnie D. Lipschutz

Pondering Postinternationalism: A Paradigm for the Twenty-First Century?—Heidi H. Hobbs (ed.)

Beyond Boundaries? Disciplines, Paradigms, and Theoretical Integration in International Studies—Rudra Sil and Eileen M. Doherty (eds.)

Why Movements Matter: The West German Peace Movement and U.S. Arms Control Policy—Steve Breyman

International Relations—Still an American Social Science? Toward Diversity in International Thought—Robert M. A. Crawford and Darryl S. L. Jarvis (eds.)

Which Lessons Matter? American Foreign Policy Decision Making in the Middle East, 1979—1987—Christopher Hemmer (ed.)

Hierarchy Amidst Anarchy: Transaction Costs and Institutional Choice—Katja Weber

Counter-Hegemony and Foreign Policy: The Dialectics of Marginalized and Global Forces in Jamaica—Randolph B. Persaud

Global Limits: Immanuel Kant, International Relations, and Critique of World Politics—Mark F. N. Franke

Power and Ideas: North-South Politics of Intellectual Property and Antitrust—Susan K. Sell

Money and Power in Europe: The Political Economy of European Monetary Cooperation—Matthias Kaelberer

Agency and Ethics: The Politics of Military Intervention—Anthony F. Lang Jr.

Life After the Soviet Union: The Newly Independent Republics of the Transcaucasus and Central Asia—Nozar Alaolmolki

Theories of International Cooperation and the Primacy of Anarchy: Explaining U.S. International Monetary Policy-Making after Bretton Woods—Jennifer Sterling-Folker

Information Technologies and Global Politics: The Changing Scope of Power and Governance—James N. Rosenau and J. P. Singh (eds.)

Technology, Democracy, and Development: International Conflict and Cooperation in the Information Age—Juliann Emmons Allison (ed.)

The Arab-Israeli Conflict Transformed: Fifty Years of Interstate and Ethnic Crises—Hemda Ben-Yehuda and Shmuel Sandler

Systems of Violence: The Political Economy of War and Peace in Colombia—Nazih Richani

Debating the Global Financial Architecture—Leslie Elliot Armijo

Political Space: Frontiers of Change and Governance in a Globalizing World—Yale Ferguson and R. J. Barry Jones (eds.)

Crisis Theory and World Order: Heideggerian Reflections—Norman K. Swazo

Political Identity and Social Change: The Remaking of the South African Social Order—Jamie Frueh

Social Construction and the Logic of Money: Financial Predominance and International Economic Leadership—J. Samuel Barkin

What Moves Man: The Realist Theory of International Relations and Its Judgment of Human Nature—Annette Freyberg-Inan

Democratizing Global Politics: Discourse Norms, International Regimes, and Political Community—Rodger A. Payne and Nayef H. Samhat

Collective Preventative Diplomacy: A Study of International Management—*Barry H. Steiner*